WINNING
LIBRARY GRANTS
A GAME PLAN

WINNING
LIBRARY GRANTS
A GAME PLAN

Herbert B. Landau

American Library Association
Chicago   2011

Herbert B. Landau is executive director of the Lancaster Public Library and its Leola and Mountville branches, in Pennsylvania. Prior to this he was director of the Milanof-Schock Library in Mount Joy, Pennsylvania. Under his leadership, the Milanof-Schock Library received AARP's Award of Excellence for Library Services for Older Adults in 2005, 2006, and 2009. In 2006 the library was named the Best Small Library in America by *Library Journal* and the Bill & Melinda Gates Foundation. Landau has more than thirty years of experience in libraries, management, publishing, marketing of scholarly and professional information, proposal writing, and contract management. He is the author of *The Small Public Library Survival Guide: Thriving on Less* (2008).

Printed in the United States of America

15 14 13 12 11   5 4 3 2 1

While extensive effort has gone into ensuring the reliability of the information in this book, the publisher makes no warranty, express or implied, with respect to the material contained herein.

Note that any URLs referenced in this volume, which were valid at the time of first print publication, may have changed prior to electronic publication.

ISBN: 978-0-8389-1047-4

Library of Congress Cataloging-in-Publication Data
Landau, Herbert B.
    Winning library grants : a game plan / Herbert B. Landau.
        p. cm.
    Includes bibliographical references and index.
    ISBN 978-0-8389-1047-4 (alk. paper)
    1. Proposal writing in library science—United States. 2. Proposal writing for grants—United States. 3. Library fund raising–United States. I. Title.
    Z683.2.U6L36 2011
    025.1'1—dc22   2010013231

Cover design by Chris Keech. Text design in Electra LH and Avenir by Dianne M. Rooney.

♾ This paper meets the requirements of ANSI/NISO Z39.48-1992 (Permanence of Paper).

ALA Editions also publishes its books in a variety of electronic formats. For more information, visit the ALA Store at www.alastore.ala.org and select eEditions.

Contents

Figures

You Too Can Be a
Successful Grant Winner

Always listen to your momma! Mine told me to pay attention in school and on the job because, she advised, everything I learned might prove to be of some use in my later life. I found this adage to be true. As a born-again public librarian, I was called upon to write grant proposals employing skills I had acquired twenty years before when I was a "Beltway bandit" (aka a government contractor). I started my career as a conventional librarian who was educated at the very traditional and first graduate library school in the United States, the Columbia University School of Library Service (founded in 1899 by none other than Melvil Dewey). However, after a stint as a special librarian in industry, I left the library world to become a systems analyst and consultant with a computer systems-oriented government-contracting firm. Early in that job I learned that a requisite to success and survival in the firm was to become skilled in marketing and, in particular, in the writing of contract and grant proposals. Another important survival skill I developed there was learning to successfully manage the projects that the winning proposals yielded. During my eleven years in that job (and in a few related positions thereafter), I estimate that I wrote several hundred proposals and supervised the writing of several hundred more. My team and I won and managed scores of contracts and grants of almost every size and shape for government agencies, not-for-profits, industrial firms, and academic institutions in the United States and even a few in foreign countries. Upon returning to my roots as a public library director in 2002, I discovered that the ability to write successful proposals and win grants could be a useful asset in my new milieu. Alas, my public library was typically short on funds and long on needs. While seeking ways to satisfy my library's special needs, I concluded that grants might be a source of needed cash and other resources. I therefore dusted off my proposal-writing skills and decided to try my hand at winning grants for my small rural public library. To my surprise (and also, I think, to that of my board and staff), my library won the first two grant proposals I wrote for it. These were a $46,000 Library Services and Technology Act (LSTA) grant to deliver library services to seniors and the homebound and a $10,000 grant from a local foundation to buy library shelving. These successes got me hooked on grant writing early in my public library career. Since then, my public library has won two more LSTA grants and many other grants from a variety of sources, with values totaling well into the six figures.

In my prior book, *The Small Public Library Survival Guide*, I explained how I discovered that the marketing techniques I had employed in industry could also work in a public library environment.[1] Similarly, my early success in winning grants for my small public library demonstrated that the proposal and contract management techniques I had learned and employed in my industry "Beltway bandit" days were adaptable to library grant writing. However, when I encouraged my fellow librarians to attempt grant writing, I found many of them were loathe to try it. They seemed to view the pursuit of grants as some arcane art far beyond their capabilities and believed that "nobody would give a grant to a small public library like mine." In fact, at one library system meeting I attended, it was suggested that the only way a small library could win a grant was to hire an expensive "professional grant writer." I have seen library consortia consider offering annual salaries up to $75,000 for an in-house grants advisor. I also receive ads from companies who offer to write a foundation or government grant proposal for me (purpose optional) for about $500–600.

Phooey on all this, I say! My personal view is that delegating your grant writing to someone outside of your library is not the best approach. You are your own best grant writer. This book is designed to dispel the unfortunate misperception among many librarians that winning grants on their own is an impossible dream. In this book I approach grant seeking as a form of marketing. I hope to demystify the grant-seeking (and -winning) process by presenting it as the logical definition of your institution and its needs and then marketing your needs to those who can fund them. Further, as many experienced grant writers will tell you, writing a grant proposal can be a therapeutic self-evaluation exercise which forces you to focus on your institution's mission and goals. I believe that no outsider can write a grant proposal as effectively as a "library insider" who fully understands your institution's mission and needs. However, if you still feel you must hire an outside consultant to aid you in your grant writing or to provide advice on certain skills your organization lacks, then heed the advice of Gerding and MacKellar:[2]

> Do not attempt to have the (outside) grant writer plan, design and write your proposal for you. This may result in a project . . . that may not be something you and your staff can or want to do. Hiring or relying on an outside grant consultant should not relieve the library of devoting time to planning a project and overseeing the design and writing of a proposal.

My premise is that virtually any librarian or library trustee can become a successful grant writer by applying a little writing skill, some marketing savvy, and a few drops of imagination to the commonsense techniques I cover in this book. I have tested this thesis in my own library, where I have trained several of my staff to also become successful *grantsmen* and *grantswomen*. You can be one too!

In this book, I introduce the reader to the basic principles and jargon of grantsmanship, discuss typical grant sources, and advise on how to identify and evaluate grant opportunities. I will then delve into the mechanics of organizing a successful grant-seeking effort, including the definition of your proposed project's scope and resource requirements, proposal organization and preparation, and proposal submission and marketing. Post-proposal tips will include advice on grant project start-up, project management, and how to learn from your wins and losses. Although this book mentions many granting agencies as examples, it should not be considered as a comprehensive guide to available grant opportunities. Comprehensive guides are discussed in chapter 4. I do, however, include both a bibliography and webliography listing the available print and online guides to library grants that I was able to identify at the time of writing.

Although the focus of this book is primarily on the needs of public libraries, the approaches and techniques presented are generic enough to work equally well for any type of grant-seeking library or for any other type of grant-seeking organization.

NOTES

1. Herbert B. Landau, *The Small Public Library Survival Guide: Thriving on Less* (Chicago: American Library Association, 2008).

2. Stephanie K. Gerding and Pamela H. MacKellar, *Grants for Libraries* (New York: Neal-Schuman, 2006), 84.

Grantsmanship Fundamentals, Definitions, and Rules

WHAT IS A "GRANT"?

Simple definitions of *grant* found in dictionaries are "to bestow," "to confer," and "to give." A "grant" can also mean "something given." Therefore, in the context of this book, let us consider a "grant" as a gift. The gift can be in the form of money, goods, or services. Noncash grants are often known as "grants-in-kind." In this book, a grantsman (aka "grantswoman") refers to one who is skilled in the art of winning grants. A grant to a library can be for a stated purpose as agreed to by the grantor and grantee (a "nondiscretionary grant"), or it can be used at the pleasure of the grantee (a "discretionary grant"). Therefore, a nondiscretionary grant may be considered as a donation with a specific purpose in mind (i.e., a "project"). In most cases the use of the granted funds or goods is usually governed by a set of rules. A "matching grant" is where a grantor provides only a portion of a project's total costs and the grantee must demonstrate that it can cover the remaining project expenses. A "competitive grant" is where the grantor sets aside a fixed amount of money and multiple libraries apply for a portion of that money. The libraries with the greatest need or the best proposal applications are then awarded portions of the total grant money. You have to *compete* for the money available, and some win grant money and some do not.

Grant vs. Contract

A "contract" differs from a "grant," although both usually require proposals and a grant project may require a formal contractual agreement between grantor and grantee. Grant projects differ from typical client/contractor projects in that the grant project's purpose is to benefit the grantee (or the patrons the grantee serves), while in a "contract" project the contractor works to benefit the client (i.e., the one who pays).

Grants Nomenclature

An organization seeking a grant may be known variously as a "grantee," "grant seeker," "donee," or "beneficiary." The prospective grantee will identify a potential grant source, known as a "grantor," "grant maker," "funder," "donor," or "benefactor," and will prepare (or "write a grant" in the current jargon) and submit a "grant request," "grant application," or "grant proposal" to the grantor. The grant process may be reactive if initiated by the grantor who issues a notice of grant opportunity known as a "request for proposal" (RFP), "invitation," or "solicitation." A "competitive grant" opportunity is where a grantor allocates a fixed amount of money for a specific purpose, publishes an RFP announcing this, and invites many prospective grantees to submit competitive proposals. Competitive proposals are evaluated by one or more reviewers (sometimes called "grant readers"), and only one or a few proposals are selected to receive a grant. Typical odds in winning a competitive grant are about one in ten. A proposal submitted in response to an RFP is known as a "solicited proposal."

On the other hand, a prospective grantee may be proactive and initiate the process by requesting a grant from a prospective grantor even though no RFP has been issued. This is known as submitting an "unsolicited proposal." Typically, government agencies and large foundations issue formal RFPs as their preferred mode of identifying deserving grantees. Smaller foundations, corporations, and individual philanthropists may be willing to consider unsolicited proposals from those seeking grants. Furthermore, some local and family foundations and individual philanthropists have been known to make unsolicited grants to libraries as part of their ongoing programs to support worthy community activities. For example, my library regularly receives small (i.e., $1,000–5,000) grants from local family foundations without asking for them. A later chapter will provide advice on how to connect with this type of grantor.

CATEGORIES OF GRANTS

Grants come in many varieties and are usually classified as to purpose or limits. While there is no standard nomenclature for grants, the excellent glossary found in the Nonprofit Good Practice Guide of the Johnson Center at Grand Valley State University (www.npgoodpractice.org/Glossary/Default.aspx?term=grant) contains many grant-related definitions among its 2,680 defined terms, including definitions of twenty different types of grants. The types of grants listed below are the typical categories that may be of interest to not-for-profit grant seekers:

Block grant—a lump sum of grant money with only general provisions as to the way it is to be spent

Building or renovation grant—a grant for constructing, renovating, remodeling, or rehabilitating property

Capacity-building grant—a grant for expanding the service capacity of the applicant

Capital grant—a grant for purchasing tangible goods (e.g., buildings, vehicles, hardware, etc.). It is usually for significant amounts of cash.

Categorical grant—a sum of grant money which has strict and specific provisions on how it is to be spent

Challenge grant—a grant that requires the grantee to raise a specified amount of additional funds from other sources. It is used to stimulate giving from others.

Demonstration grant—a grant used to prove or disprove (test) a concept or theory prior to major funding

Endowment grant—a grant of funds to be invested, with the income to benefit a specific institution or purpose

Evaluation grant—a grant that supports the external evaluation of a project or projects

Grant-in-aid—a gift of funds to an institution or a person in order to subsidize a project or program

Grant-in-kind—a gift of goods or services, rather than cash

Matching grant—a grant made to match funds from the grantee or another source; a grant made in response to a challenge grant

Multiyear grant—a commitment by a grantor to provide support for more than one year (typically two to five years), contingent upon satisfactory grantee performance

Operational grant—a grant used to support basic ongoing activities; it is also known as a core funding grant, operating support grant, or general support grant

Performance or production grant—a grant used to cover costs specifically associated with mounting performing arts productions

Planning grant—a grant that supports such efforts as goal setting, information gathering, needs assessment, coalition building, or planning for a larger grant

Program or project grant—a grant to achieve a specific project-related outcome or deliverable within a specific time frame, as opposed to general purpose grants

Research grant—a grant awarded to an institution to cover the costs of investigation and laboratory or clinical trials. Research grants to individuals are usually referred to as fellowships.

Restricted grant—a grant made to an organization for a particular project or purpose. The funds may be used only for the purpose designated by the grantor.

Special project grant—a grant to support the costs associated with a particular project rather than the organization as a whole

Start-up or seed money grant—a grant used to assist an institution in initiating an activity, with sustainable funding to be obtained from other sources

Supplemental or supplementary grant—a commitment made to augment an existing grant commitment; it is also called an add-on grant

Sustainability grant—a grant to sustain a service or project

Technical assistance grant—a monetary grant or in-kind contribution for management assistance to help a nonprofit organization operate more effectively. Accounting, consulting, financial planning, fund-raising, and legal support are some common types of technical assistance.

Youth grant making—programs that involve young people in the process of grant making, usually for youth-related projects

THE TWENTY-FIVE STEPS
OF THE GRANTSMANSHIP CYCLE

There are basically twenty-five stepping-stones along the path to being a successful grantsman, as shown in figure 2.1. These can be divided up into five distinct stages:

FIGURE 2.1

TWENTY-FIVE STEPS TO GRANT SEEKING AND WINNING

I. Pre-proposal Market Analysis and Proposal Planning
 1. Verify your institution's resolve, resources, and eligibility to be a successful grant seeker
 2. Find a grantor whose mission and scope match your need
 3. Establish pre-proposal marketing contact
 4. Obtain grant application details (e.g., an RFP)
 5. Study and analyze the grant submission rules
 6. Conduct preliminary research and fact-finding
 7. Make go/no-go proposal decision

II. Proposal Management and Project Planning
 1. Do research and fact-finding
 2. Establish application proposal writing and delivery schedule
 3. Logically outline your project
 4. Logically outline your proposal
 5. Define your proposal budget and obtain funds
 6. Organize your proposal-writing team and resources
 7. Seek strong complementary partners (optional)

III. Proposal Writing
 1. Prepare the proposal application
 2. Follow a logical proposal outline

IV. Proposal Assembly, Editing, Review, and Submission
 1. Review the application proposal package
 2. Submit the application proposal

V. Post-proposal Marketing and Project Initiation
 1. Follow-up communication
 2. Loss debriefing (if appropriate)
 3. Contract execution
 4. Kickoff meeting
 5. Project task initiation
 6. Grant reporting
 7. Ensuring sustainability

I. Pre-proposal Market Analysis and Proposal Planning

II. Proposal Management and Project Planning

III. Proposal Writing

IV. Proposal Assembly, Editing, Review, and Submission

V. Post-proposal Marketing and Project Initiation

Each of these phases and steps will be developed in the following chapters of this book. Not all of these twenty-five steps will be applicable to all grant situations, so you may have to mix and match the steps that best suit your institution and the particular situation.

LANDAU'S TEN RULES
OF SUCCESSFUL GRANTSMANSHIP

When playing in a game, it helps to have a set of rules to go by. To assist myself in winning at the library grants game, I have developed a set of ten commonsense rules over the years by which I govern my proposal plays:

1. Pursue only grants relevant to your institution's mission.

2. Do not pursue a grant if proposal preparation costs are more than the grant is worth.

3. Do not pursue a grant opportunity if the odds against winning are more than ten to one.

4. Appoint a reliable proposal manager.

5. Find compatible partners to provide needed skills or eligibility.

6. Read the proposal instructions and give them exactly what they want.

7. Meet your proposal submission deadline.

8. Don't be a pest to the grantor.

9. Follow the grantor's contract rules.

10. Do not continue to pursue lost causes.

The application of these rules will be discussed in the relevant chapters of this book that follow.

Pre-proposal Market Analysis and Planning

ven before you start obtaining and analyzing grant RFPs and visiting prospective grantors, you must determine if your institution is ready to embark on the grant-seeking trail.

VERIFYING YOUR INSTITUTION'S RESOLVE, RESOURCES, AND ELIGIBILITY TO BE A SUCCESSFUL GRANT SEEKER

I do not recommend pursuing grants just for the sake of competition, although the excitement of the chase can be exhilarating once you become comfortable with your grant-writing skills. Writing a grant is serious work and can take a significant amount of time and effort that can become a drain on a public library's core activities, staff, and resources. Writing competitive grants can be a gamble with no guarantee of a payoff for the effort invested.

To be successful as a grant seeker, your institution will need to be sure that it can satisfy several necessary conditions. These are:

- ◆ The grant project supports your institutional mission and priorities.
- ◆ You possess the resolve, eligibility, institutional structure, and institutional support for grant seeking.

- ◆ You possess appropriate and available institutional resources and skills to seek and identify grant opportunities.

- ◆ You possess appropriate and available institutional resources and skills to prepare and submit a grant proposal.

- ◆ You possess appropriate and available institutional resources and skills to successfully manage a grant project.

- ◆ You can stand up against the competition.

- ◆ You have enough time to prepare a winning proposal.

To decide if grant seeking is an opportunity for your institution, you can employ a grant decision tree, such as that illustrated in figure 3.1. You can use this to ask yourself a series of go/no-go questions to determine if it makes sense to pursue grants in general. Each of these critical considerations in deciding to pursue grants is discussed below.

PURSUE ONLY GRANTS RELEVANT TO YOUR INSTITUTION'S MISSION

My rule number 1 of grant writing is: *Pursue only grants relevant to your institution's mission.* Pursue only useful, relevant, and timely grants. There is scant value in conducting a grant project that contributes little towards the achievement of your library's priority goals and objectives. Therefore, as you peruse grant opportunities that may come your way, the very first question to ask is: "Will the prospective grant project contribute any real benefits to my library and its services to patrons?" If you cannot answer this question with a resounding yes, then it is best to let the grant opportunity pass.

The Grantsmanship Center's Patty Hasselbring cautions grant seekers against falling prey to "mission creep."[1] This is where a prospective grantee begins to "chase the money" and create proposals that fit only the needs of the funder, rather than seeking projects that fulfill the grantee's mission and meet its needs. She states that a reactive approach to grant seeking can cause an institution to lose its mission focus, with negative consequences. Her proposed solution is to always remember your library's mission and its priorities in seeking grants.

Your library's strategic plan should be the basis for clarifying your library's potentially grantable needs. Use your plan's stated mission, objectives, goals, and strategic tasks as input to your grant-shopping list. This can help to avoid the pursuit of potentially "frivolous" grants and can also help you to justify and

FIGURE 3.1

GRANT DECISION TREE

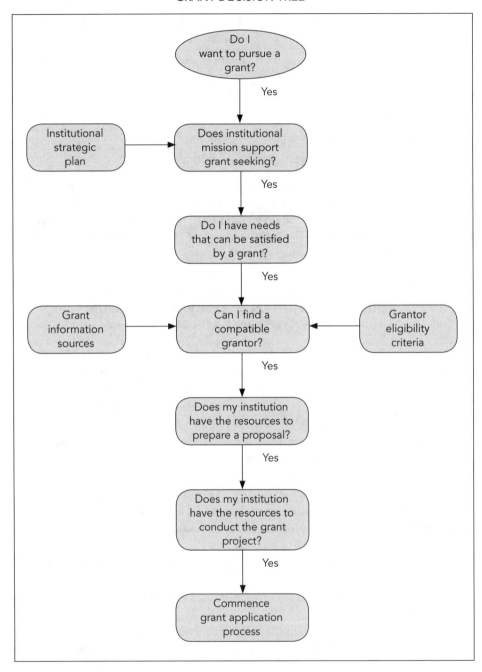

validate the investment of library resources in grant-seeking efforts to your library's governing body. Relating grant seeking to your strategic plan is also important because grantors often now ask applicants to submit their relevant strategic plan segments as part of the grant application package. For example, Pennsylvania's LSTA grant applications now mandate the submission of germane strategic plan chapters as part of the grant seeker's proposal.

After you conclude that grant seeking is compatible with your institution's mission and scope, you still have to face a number of "go/no-go" decision points before a grant proposal is written and submitted. The *grant decision tree* in figure 3.1 and the following chapters of this book are designed to help you make these difficult decisions and to guide you in preparing a solid, competitive grant application proposal when you decide to "go for the grant."

ESTABLISHING YOUR GRANT "MISSION MATCH"

To be a successful grantsman or grantswoman, you will need to successfully demonstrate two degrees of mission matching in your grant-seeking proposals:

♦ Matching your institution's mission with the grantor's mission

♦ Matching the project's mission with your institution's mission and the grantor's mission

For example, when my public library's children's game computers wore out and needed replacement, we identified and approached a local family foundation whose mission supported the use of technology to aid learning for children and youth. In our unsolicited proposal to them we demonstrated first that our public library was dedicated to serving the community's lifelong learning needs, including those of children and youth. We then made a case for how a pair of new children-friendly computer workstations, loaded with approved educational tools and games, would contribute to the development of early learning skills. As a result, we won a $5,000 grant. In another instance, a local community foundation advertised that they would entertain grant requests in support of their mission to improve literacy and the appreciation of reading. In our proposal responding to this, we showed that our library's mission specifically includes serving the reading needs of our service area's residents. We emphasized this by listing as evidence the many preschool, juvenile, young adult, and adult reading programs and events we regularly offer. Then we requested grant funding for a series of teen poetry and short story-writing workshops. We directly linked the goals of this project to the missions of both the library and the foundation (i.e., to encourage literacy, appreciation of literature, and the development of writing skills). We were awarded a $3,800 grant as a result.

Do not be shy or oblique in demonstrating your mission match. Come right out and state that "the mission (or goals) of this proposed project and its expected outcomes will directly support the stated mission of the XYZ Foundation in the following ways: . . ."

DETERMINING IF YOUR ORGANIZATION IS ELIGIBLE FOR A GRANT

Most philanthropic and government grant makers limit specific grants to a particular category of grantee such as an individual, a business, or a not-for-profit institution. Determine these limitations in advance so you will not waste effort in applying for a grant that you are not eligible to win.

Grants to Individuals

Grant funding to individuals is very limited. However, there are certain grants that are awarded by foundations, corporations, or governments to individuals for education or for research or innovation in science, the arts, and the humanities. In addition, there are two finding tools from the Foundation Center in New York, the *PND RFP Bulletin* and the Foundation Grants to Individuals Online database, which list grant opportunities for individuals. More on the Foundation Center and its activities in support of grant seekers can be found in chapter 4.

Grants to Businesses

Most grants are reserved for not-for-profit organizations and are only rarely awarded to for-profit firms. The federal government's official business website, Business.gov (www.business.gov/finance/financing/grants), candidly tells us:

> We've all seen the headlines: "Millions in free government money for your business." Late-night infomercials and Internet advertisements promise grants to start or expand a business. Sounds too good to be true? It is. The federal government does not provide grants for starting and expanding a business. Grants from the federal government are only available to non-commercial organizations, such as non-profits and educational institutions . . . Some business grants are available through state and local programs, non-profit organizations and other groups [but] . . . these grants are not necessarily free

money, and usually require the recipient to match funds or combine the grant with other forms of financing such as a loan.

Grants to Not-for-Profit Organizations

The vast majority of available grant opportunities are reserved for not-for-profit institutional entities that have been granted 501(c)(3) tax-exempt status by the U.S. Internal Revenue Service (IRS). To qualify for this status, your organization must submit to the IRS a completed Form 1023 or 1024, Application for Recognition of Exemption Under Section 501(c)(3) of the Internal Revenue Code. If approved, you will receive a "tax determination letter" from the IRS confirming your not-for-profit status; that is, your institution is what is known as a "501(c)(3) organization." Keep this determination letter handy, for, often as not, you will have to submit a copy of it in a grant application as evidence of your eligibility.

Although they are not-for-profit, certain agencies that are considered as governmental departments may be barred from applying to certain granting bodies or may be prevented by doing so by their own parent bodies or by enabling documents. In addition, many foundations or government agencies do not offer grants to religious or political action organizations. Therefore, before investing time and effort in grant seeking, it is prudent to first verify that your institution's enabling documents (e.g., articles of incorporation, bylaws, legislative and taxing authority, etc.) allow you to seek and accept grants. Further, when evaluating certain grant opportunities, you should first verify that an organization such as yours meets the grantor's standards of eligibility. For example, my library was interested in exploring grant opportunities with a local business foundation that had a history of supporting not-for-profit institutions. However, upon inquiring about their eligibility criteria, we learned that they limited their support to faith-based institutions and, therefore, as a public library we did not qualify.

Do You Need a Partner to Provide Complimentary or Necessary Qualifications?

If you do not meet the grantor's conditions to qualify or if your organization is weak in certain requisite project areas, you may still be able to benefit from grant funding by partnering with another grant-qualified agency in submitting a joint grant proposal. My public library has partnered in grant seeking with a university, a municipality, a museum, and an association for the restoration of historic buildings. See chapter 8 for advice on selecting and working with grant partners.

CAN YOU COMMIT THE RESOURCES NECESSARY TO IDENTIFY GRANT OPPORTUNITIES AND TO SUBMIT A WINNING GRANT PROPOSAL?

Wanting to win a grant is not enough. A successful grant seeker must possess and be willing to commit the manpower and resources necessary both to find relevant grant opportunities and then to write a winning grant proposal. One has to find and commit the necessary effort to the pre-proposal and proposal efforts outlined below, such as searching grantor databases and reference books to identify "prospects," visiting prospective grantors, writing letters of inquiry, attending pre-proposal workshops, seeking partners, and so on. Your management staff and governing body will have to set aside time to meet and deliberate over whether or not the risks vs. benefits of a grant opportunity warrant its pursuit and who will contribute needed resources to the proposal effort. Therefore, it is important to obtain the support of your institution's governing body, be it an independent board or a city council, for your grant-seeking efforts at two levels:

1. Support for committing institutional resources to grant seeking in general
2. Support for specific grant-seeking efforts if they will consume significant resources at either the proposal preparation or post-award project stages

A major grant proposal effort can require a significant investment of time and money in planning, proposal preparation, and obtaining expert advice. For example, the average government grant request can take from 80 to 160 person-hours to write, plus additional effort devoted to logistical and marketing support tasks. A senior and qualified staff member will have to be detailed to serve as proposal manager. She must then create a proposal schedule and plan and must recruit a team of proposal contributors who possess the necessary writing and subject expertise and who can devote whatever time is needed to meet the deadline. Outside expert consultants (such as architects and engineers for a construction project) may have to be hired and paid. Quotations from outside vendors (for material such as computers) may have to be solicited. Editors and graphic designers may be needed to design, assemble, and review the proposal documents. Budget specialists may be needed to prepare the cost estimates. A print shop may be needed to produce the hard-copy proposal, a courier service may be needed to deliver it on time, and so on. All of these proposal tasks can be a drain on the grant-seeking institution's staff and financial resources. Therefore, before you start grant seeking, verify that your institution has the necessary means available and is able to invest the labor, cash, and other resources needed to generate winning grant proposals. In determining how much you may need to invest in a grant proposal preparation effort, consider my grant rule number 2: *Do not pursue a grant if the proposal preparation costs more than the grant is worth.*

Similarly, one should also look down the road and ask if your institution possesses (or can readily obtain) the resources necessary to successfully conduct and sustain a grant project should you win it. Most grants are for programs or projects that are new initiatives rather than for the support of ongoing base operations. Therefore, if winning a major grant requires either the reassignment of current staff or the allocation of additional staff and facilities, this can negatively affect your core operations if you are not prepared to handle the additional work.

ARE THE ODDS OF WINNING A GRANT FAVORABLE?

Writing competitive grants can be a gamble, with no guarantee of a payoff for the effort invested. Typically, the chances of winning a grant competition can be as low as one in ten and even lower in some instances. In evaluating the odds of winning a grant, I therefore apply my rule number 3 of successful grantsmanship: *Do not pursue a grant opportunity if the odds against winning are more than ten to one.* For example, in 2009 the International City/County Management Association, with Gates Foundation backing, advertised a grant competition to fund public library/municipality cooperative projects. Although 515 joint library/municipal applications were submitted, only nine winning grants were awarded! With odds against winning of greater than 57 to 1, this is the type of grant competition whose odds against winning make it not worth pursuing, in my view.

CREATING AN INSTITUTIONAL FOCAL POINT FOR YOUR GRANT-WRITING EFFORTS

As this book shows, grant seeking and proposal writing, though sometimes fun, can also be hard work, requiring that certain institutional skills be developed. It is therefore important to establish a focal point within your library for seeking, considering, and responding to grant opportunities. Diana L. Megdad is the keystone library facilities advisor for the Pennsylvania Commonwealth Libraries, and she oversees the awarding and administration of millions of dollars in public library construction grants each year. She frequently provides advice to library grant seekers in Pennsylvania, and her e-mail advisory of July 17, 2009, addresses this issue when she asks:

Are you a small library without a *development office?* Is the library director doing it all—as well as researching and writing grants? Think about getting some free help if you can't afford to hire a grant writer! Or, perhaps several libraries can go together and share someone. Put out a call in your community for someone who could assist in writing grants. It should be seen as a high-prestige volunteer position and advertised as such (word of mouth or put an ad in the paper!). A *job description is essential* (all volunteers should have one) and you can *be selective!* They have the satisfaction of helping the library and personal publicity when the grants start rolling in! This volunteer can be on the lookout for appropriate grants and do most of the legwork. The librarian will still need to give input and do some work, but it will cut down on missed opportunities and passing up grants due to too little time.

My view is that the person in the grant development position that Megdad defines above is a marketer who seeks out grant opportunities, does database research, monitors federal grant opportunities, attends grant workshops, obtains and evaluates interesting RFPs, and maintains relationships and negotiates with potential grantors. This type of work requires knowledge of market analysis, public relations, selling, negotiating, and letter writing, all very important marketing skills. In addition to these classic marketing skills, proposal management and preparation also require a management skill mix of organizational, budgeting, planning, and technical writing abilities as further discussed in chapter 8. If you can find a marketing-oriented person who is also a good proposal manager and writer to serve as your grant development officer, then you are blessed. If not, it may be necessary to employ your grant development officer more as a bird dog to sniff out and locate grant opportunities. You can then employ another person as grant proposal manager, or the hunter who will provide the weapons to bag and take home the elusive grant funds you are seeking. In any case, both functions are closely related and must be integrated.

EMPLOYING BOARD MEMBERS AND VOLUNTEERS TO HELP WIN GRANTS

Of course, you must make sure that you have the support of your board of trustees for your grant-seeking activities. Keep your board apprised of your grant hunting and co-opt them to your grant-writing team if they can contribute knowledge or skills. Board members can also be invaluable in helping with the bird-dogging investigative legwork preliminary to obtaining grants from foundation, corporate, and even government funders. Jeannette Archer-Simons suggests giving trustees some of the responsibility for research, such as using their contacts and experience to identify foundations that are likely to support your organization or gathering statistics and demographic data to use in proposals.[2] Invite your trustees to ask their business associates, friends, and colleagues at corporations, bank trust departments, investment firms, and government agencies about possible grant sources. As ambassadors for your organization, board members can open doors for you. Just make sure they have been provided with talking points to use in selling your library when they are out in the community, attending meetings, or accompanying your library director on visits to grant makers.

Organizations short on development staff can also look to volunteers for help in securing grants. If you can't afford to hire a paid development staffer, or if the staff person who identifies grant opportunities and writes proposals is swamped with other responsibilities, consider using a volunteer. In "Building Your Grants Team with Inside and Outside Volunteers" (CharityChannel, April 15, 2009), Lynne T. Dean recommends asking volunteers who are self-motivated to search the Internet for grant sources. For proposal writing, tap volunteers who are experienced writers, can adopt different styles, and can work under deadline pressure.

CREATING AN INSTITUTIONAL GRANT RESOURCES FILE

Pennsylvania Commonwealth Libraries' Megdad advises us to set up a resource file of materials to be included in grant proposals when she states in her e-mail advisory of July 17, 2009: "Many grants ask for the same things—they want a copy of your 990 or your mission statement, demographics, etc. When time or a volunteer's availability allows, gather multiple copies of these items in one place for ready accessibility when a grant opportunity presents itself." If your organization becomes a regular grant seeker, you can avoid repetition and save a lot of time by creating a grant resources file, or, as the pros call it, a "boilerplate" file. This boilerplate should include items that are regularly required in grant proposals such as

- ◆ a concise overview description of your organization and its role in the community
- ◆ board roster with affiliations
- ◆ IRS 501(c)(3) tax-exempt determination letter
- ◆ latest IRS 990 annual filing

- last five years of annual audited financial reports
- current and prior year's annual operating budgets
- annual reports
- organization chart
- one-page biographies of all key staff members
- articles of incorporation and bylaws
- anti-discrimination policy (for government grants)
- mission statement and strategic plan
- letters of support
- awards and special achievements
- favorable media clippings
- photos of program activities and facilities
- prior grant proposals

An important asset in your grant resources file will be the grant proposals you have already written.

In some cases you will find that certain sections, such as qualifications, organizational background, and so on may be recycled and used in future proposals by cutting and pasting. These can also serve as instructional models to train new proposal writers on your staff. Templates for standard proposal elements such as cover letters, cover pages, tables of contents, staff biographies, and so on can also be useful resources in this file.

NOTES

1. Patty Hasselbring, "7 Steps to Warding Off Mission Creep," *Centered* (newsletter of the Grantsmanship Center) 1, no. 3 (September 2008): 1–3.

2. Jeanette Archer-Simons, "Board Members as Grants Advocates," CharityChannel, March 4, 2009, www.charitychannel.com.

Finding Grants
and Granting Organizations
Relevant to Libraries

Matchmaking, that is, finding a compatible grantor to whom you can apply for funding, is half the battle in becoming a grants-man or grantswoman. Comparing the respective missions of grantors is a good place to start.

MISSION MATCHING: FINDING THE GRANTOR WHOSE MISSION AND SCOPE MATCH YOUR NEEDS

Let's start with the basics to help you focus on your grant needs. A grantor is an organization or individual that has a need to give away funds in line with a stated mission. A grantee is an organization or individual that has a need to receive funds to support a stated mission. Therefore, the art of successful grantsmanship is to match your institution's need to receive with another's need to give. I call this establishing a "mission match." The first step, then, is to define and classify your library's needs so you can identify and apply to grantor organizations whose giving focus is compatible with your needs focus. For example, both the Bill & Melinda Gates Foundation's grants and a state's LSTA grants tend to focus on the application of technology by libraries to satisfy the needs of library patrons. Therefore, if your library's needs involve technology applications, these are two grant sources to investigate. Some granting foundations focus on services to special population groups such as children, minorities, seniors, or the handicapped. Some government grants are set aside specifically for library construction or renovation. Therefore, first clarify and prioritize your library's needs and then focus on grant agencies whose giving focus is in line with your needs. You don't want to waste your time writing a grant proposal to an organization that may reject it out of hand for being beyond the organization's scope of interest.

The remainder of this chapter outlines research tools useful in identifying and analyzing grant funders by the categories of foundations, corporations, associations, and the various levels of government. This chapter, along with the bibliography and webliography, identifies information sources that will help you to identify grant opportunities.

FOUNDATIONS AND INDIVIDUAL PHILANTHROPISTS

Foundations (both private and corporate) have become a primary source of public library grants. Deborah Ward divides foundations into four categories:[1]

Independent foundations—private not-for-profit funders, including family foundations

Company-sponsored foundations—foundations established and funded by assets from a for-profit business

Community foundations—foundations that raise and donate funds within specific geographic areas

Operating foundations—foundations that exist to conduct specific activities and seldom award grants

Foundations come in all sizes, from small family foundations providing moderate funding to support local causes to large organizations with international focus that give away millions of dollars. A good example of the latter is the Bill & Melinda Gates Foundation, whose current generosity towards libraries rivals that of the early twentieth-century philanthropist Andrew Carnegie. Community foundations normally make their charitable grants within a specific geographical region. Occasionally, individual philanthropists and corporations will offer to fund projects in areas of interest to them, but it is becoming more common for them to create foundations through which they channel their grant funding. The Foundation Center's information dissemination and database services (see below) do, however, list grant RFPs from individuals and corporations as well as foundations.

SCOPE OF FOUNDATION GRANT SOURCES

The American Library Association's *Big Book of Library Grant Money* lists approximately 2,400 U.S. philanthropic programs that have either made grants to libraries or have listed libraries as potential grant recipients. At the time of this writing, the Foundation Center's database listed 96,032 grant maker organizations. The Foundation Center's Statistical Information Service (www .foundationcenter.org/findfunders/statistics) tells us that in 2006, 72,477 U.S. foundations distributed 140,484 grants worth over $19.1 billion. Of these, 1,021 grants, with a value of $157,059,000, were directed specifically at libraries.

FOUNDATION GRANT INFORMATION RESOURCES

There are many foundations whose missions and purposes allow them to provide support to public libraries in need. These range from the very large, such as the Bill & Melinda Gates Foundation with hundreds of millions of dollars at its disposal, down to small local community foundations providing grants of $1,000. However, they all share one overriding characteristic: they were created to give support to worthy organizations and individuals. As stated earlier, the secret is to successfully match a foundation's need to give with your need to receive.

In selecting a foundation or any other grant opportunity to pursue, scheduling is important because most foundations and granting agencies operate on prescribed annual or even biennial grant cycles. Therefore, if you miss a cycle, you might have to wait a year or more for the next round to begin.

Foundation Center

79 Fifth Avenue, New York, NY 10003-3076; Phone: 212-620-4230
E-mail: foundationcenter.org/newyork

The best single source for information on foundation grants is the not-for-profit Foundation Center in New York City. The databases of the Foundation Center and of the similar Council on Foundations include details on more than 96,000 grant makers, and the print *Foundation Directory* lists the top 10,000 foundations in terms of giving, although not all foundations cited in these sources will provide funds to libraries. To determine which foundations, either in your area or beyond, offer grants to help libraries, you can use the Foundation Center's website (www.foundationcenter.org) and databases to help you find them. You can enter a search subject or click on the U.S. map and search by state, county, city, zip code, or congressional district. You can also search by type of recipient organization. Your search should identify the names of the potential grantors and the amount and purpose of their grants. Although a subscription is required to access many Foundation Center digital and print products, the center provides free access to all files through the Foundation Center Cooperating Collections network of libraries and nonprofit information centers throughout the United States, Mexico, and South Korea. You can locate libraries designated as "Foundation Center Cooperating Collections" at http://foundationcenter .org/collections/ccpa.html. Each library offers a core collection of publications administered by an advisory librarian. These centers also provide fund-raising information and other funding-related technical assistance in their communities and offer free funding research guidance to all visitors. Many also provide a variety of other services for local nonprofit organizations, using staff or volunteers to prepare special materials, organize workshops, or conduct orientations. As an alternative to visiting a Foundation Center Cooperating Collection, you can chat live online with a Foundation Center librarian via their online reference service at http://foundationcenter.org/getstarted/askus. Free online courses are also available at the Foundation Center: http://foundationcenter .org/getstarted/training/online, or you may attend live fee-based classes in Washington, DC, and in other cities as well. A listing of these can be found at http:// foundationcenter.org/washington/;jsessionid=4UOR3IWSJ3AIXLAQBQ4CG W15AAAACI2F.

FOUNDATION CENTER'S PHILANTHROPY NEWS DIGEST AND PND RFP BULLETIN

The Foundation Center's *Philanthropy News Digest* (PND) announces RFPs and notices of awards as a free service for grant-making organizations and nonprofits. The Foundation Center's database of grant opportunities listed in *PND* can also be accessed online at http://foundationcenter.org/pnd/rfp. A March 2009 search of this RFP database under the term *libraries* yielded a listing of ten relevant RFPs from a range of such diverse sources as the History Channel, American Library Association (ALA), Federal Institute of Museum and Library Services, a private individual philanthropist, American Association of School Librarians, Preserve America Institute of the White House, Dollar General Foundation, EDS Corporation, Laura Bush Foundation, and National Endowment for the Humanities.

At this *PND* website, you can also subscribe to the free *PND RFP Bulletin*, a spin-off of *PND* that is a weekly subject-classified e-mail listing of RFPs received by the Foundation Center. I consider this to be a particularly valuable service to keep aware of solicited grant opportunities as they occur. New RFPs are grouped under such subjects as Aging; Arts and Culture; Children and Youth; Civil and Human Rights; Education; Environment; Health; Human Services; Journalism/Media; Medical Research; Philanthropy, Religion and Voluntarism. Library-related RFPs are typically listed under "Education." You can also sign up for this awareness service via the Foundation Center's website (http://foundationcenter .org). In addition, if yours is a grantor organization, the Foundation Center will post your RFPs, in both its database and in the *PND RFP Bulletin*, at no charge if they are submitted at least four weeks before the earliest deadline date.

The *PND RFP Bulletin* notices are not necessarily limited to foundations offering scholarly grants, and often contain government and corporate solicitations. This reference service also does a good job of listing grants for individuals (as does the Foundation Center's Grants to Individuals Online database), which are not all that common. Because of the interesting and sometimes funky RFPs it lists, I really look forward to my weekly e-mail of the *PND RFP Bulletin*, and sometimes I find a treasure or two there. For example, in a May 2009 issue, I found an RFP from the Travelocity travel agency soliciting proposals from individuals for grants of $5,000 each to fund ecotourism explorations to such exotic destinations as the Kalahari Desert, the Amazon, Machu Picchu, India, Tanzania, and the national parks of the United States. I found this to be so intriguing that I personally applied to Travelocity for an Amazon trip grant. Then in a June 2009 issue, I found an RFP from Tom's of Maine (yes, the toothpaste folks) offering $20,000 Community Sponsorship Grants. I also responded to this RFP on behalf of my public library (in collaboration with a local historical restoration association) with a proposal to establish a public library branch in a restored building in the historic area of a nearby town.

Council on Foundations

2121 Crystal Drive, Suite 700, Arlington, VA 22202
Phone: 800-673-9036   Website: www.cof.org

The Council on Foundations database (www.cof.org) includes over 2,000 worldwide grant-making foundations and giving programs in its membership, including community, corporate, family, private, public, and international grant makers. Its website identifies these organizations and gives background information on each one and its grant programs. The council also holds an annual convention, which is an excellent networking opportunity for grant seekers.

Grantsmanship Center

P.O. Box 17220, Los Angeles, CA 90017; Phone: 213-482-9860
Website: http://tgci.com/abouthistory.shtml

The Grantsmanship Center offers grantsmanship training to nonprofit and government agencies and conducts about 150 workshops a year across the country. It also publishes a brief guide entitled *Program Planning and Proposal Writing*. It issues the *Grantsmanship Center Magazine*, which contains daily grant announcements from the *Federal Register*, and offers an online index of funding sources at the local, federal, and international levels. The Grantsmanship Center's online database lists federal grant programs and announcements, state funding sites, and private funders.

Technology Grant News and Grant Index

Technology Grant News; 561 Hudson Street #23
New York, NY 10014; Phone: 212-929-4347
Website: www.technologygrantnews.com

One can subscribe to this commercial publisher's quarterly print and electronic guides to grants in the area of technology for $35 (electronic) or $85 (electronic with print). Grant indexes cover these areas:

cities grants	libraries and museums
corporate grants	nonprofit grants
educational technology grants	science education grants
federal grants	university grants
higher education	vocational education grants
K–12 school grants	

Other titles available from this publisher include *Everything Technology: Directory of Technology Grants, Awards, Contests, Grants, Scholarships,* and *Winning at It: Grant Writing for Technology Grants: Corporate & Government Tech Grants, with Winning Proposals & Projects for Non-Profits; K-12 Schools, Colleges & Universities, Individuals, Awards, Fellowships with Winning Proposals, Projects*.

IRS 990 Forms as Foundation Information Sources

The IRS 990 forms can be useful sources of information on foundations. Form 990 is the Internal Revenue Service's annual Return of Organization Exempt from Income Tax, and the 990-PF form is the version to be filed by private foundations. For foundations that do not have websites or that do not issue annual reports, the IRS Form 990-PF may be your primary source of intelligence on them. Form 990-PF provides an annual definition of the foundation's mission, detailed financial data, a complete list of grants awarded, the names of the foundation's trustees and officers, and other useful information. This form may be the only source where you can find complete grants lists for smaller foundations. The amount of detail provided on each grant will vary from foundation to foundation. There are several sources of access to IRS Form 990-PF for foundations of interest. These include the five sources identified below.

The Foundation Center's Form 990 Database

The Foundation Center offers online access to Forms 990 and 990-PF via its 990 Finder online database (http://tfcny.fdncenter.org/990s/990search/esearch .php), which allows Form 990s to be searched directly online in PDF format by charity name, state, zip code, and EIN number. The Foundation Center maintains foundation Form 990s, annual reports, and other publications for the last three to four years before they are then archived at the Indiana University-Purdue University Indianapolis (IUPUI) Library. IUPUI's Foundation Center FOLIO (Foundation Literature Online) repository (https://folio.iupui.edu) goes back to 1956 and consists of four series collections: (1) IRS Tax Document Collection, (2) Historical Information Files, (3) Annual Reports (including a browsable database of holdings), and (4) Print Directories.

You can also access the Foundation Center's online Form 990 database images via the website of the National Center for Charitable Statistics at the Urban Institute (http://nccsdataweb.urban.org/PubApps/990search.php).

Internal Revenue Service

Copies of individual Forms 990-PF are also available from the IRS for a fee, using Form 4506-A, which you can request from the IRS by calling 1-800-829-8815. This service is also available on the IRS website (www.irs.gov/pub/irs-pdf/f4506a.pdf). Alternatively, you can write a letter, including the full name of the organization, its Employer Identification Number (EIN), and the year(s) needed. You should either mail or fax your requests to: Internal Revenue Service, Mail Stop 6716, Ogden, UT 84201; fax: 801-620-7896. However, since 1998 a unique public/private partnership of Philanthropic Research, Inc., the National Center for Charitable Statistics at the Urban Institute (NCCS), and the Internal Revenue Service has been digitally scanning paper Forms 990 submitted by charitable organizations. The IRS then forwards the scanned images to GuideStar and the NCCS, where they are formatted for access on the Internet. On October 18, 1999, these scanned images were posted through the websites of GuideStar (www.guidestar.org) and the NCCS (http://nccs.urban .org). Approximately 220,000 Forms 990 are accessible at no charge and are updated as new scanned images are received.

GuideStar

GuideStar is an online database of information on the activities and finances of 1.8 million nonprofit organizations, and is run by Philanthropic Research, Inc. It offers current foundation Forms 990-PF on its website. Free registration is required in order to view Forms 990-PF at GuideStar's website: www .guidestar.org.

State Attorneys General

The attorneys general of various states may have copies of Form 990-PF returns for foundations in their states. If the organization you are looking for is in California, for example, the State Attorney General's Office of California has posted nearly 90,000 California state charity and foundation tax returns (Forms 990, 990-EZ, and 990-PF) at its website (www.ag.ca.gov).

Obtaining 990s Directly from Foundations

Since 1999, the IRS has required charitable organizations to provide copies of their 990 filings on request to inquirers. Generally, the IRS Form 990 copy should be made available by the charity on the same day if the request is made in person or within thirty days in response to written requests made via regular mail, e-mail, facsimile, or private delivery. The charity is allowed to charge for actual postage plus a modest copying fee as specified in the regulation. The regulation also notes that charities that make their IRS Form 990s available on the Internet (in approved formats) are not to be required to distribute hard photocopies.

IDENTIFYING LOCAL FOUNDATIONS

When seeking to identify foundations that might provide a grant to your library, I suggest you start at the local level. This offers the greatest chance of success and the least amount of competition, although grant funding at the local level is not as great as that for the large national foundations. In addition, local foundations usually have far simpler application procedures and quicker award cycles than the major philanthropic organizations. You can identify potential local benefactors by searching the databases cited above, scanning local newspapers for notices of grant opportunities, or simply looking under the heading "Foundations–Educational, Philanthropic, Research" in your local Yellow Pages directory. Also, search the Web and regional directories to determine if there is a foundation or grant-provider directory service for your state or region, such as one we have in Pennsylvania called Pennsylvania Foundations Online (www.pafoundations.net), a subscription database service with over 2,100 profiled Pennsylvania foundations.

Once you have identified foundations whose interests and grant programs are relevant to your institution's needs, contact them and ask about their grant eligibility criteria, grant amount limits, and proposal submission and award schedules. It would not hurt to mention that your public library is classified as an IRS 501(c)(3) educational and charitable institution. For several years, my library has received modest grants from local foundations ranging from $1,500 to $10,000. Some of these grants required written applications stating a discrete need (e.g., library shelving, a children's computer, courses for seniors, etc.), while other smaller grants were available merely for the asking, with no written application being necessary. Some of the local foundation grants we received were unsolicited and were provided because our library publicity had made the foundations aware of our good works and needs. Therefore, keep the local foundations on both your publicity and solicitation mailing lists.

BUSINESS CORPORATION FOUNDATIONS

If a foundation is affiliated with a company, conduct additional research to try and uncover as much of the following information as possible by surveying and keeping up with local newspapers, business journals, chamber of commerce events, online corporate databanks, and, in some cases, fee-based services. Bernie Jankowski at Jankowski Research advises us that there are five elements of information you need to collect about business corporation-financed foundations:[2]

What is the company's size in terms of annual sales/revenues and number of employees? How healthy are its balance sheets? Is this the headquarters office or a subsidiary, branch, or affiliate location?

What are its major products, services, industry position, and/or future direction as detailed in its annual report (available online for public companies)? Many private companies also have set up websites for marketing purposes, providing researchers with easier access to this kind of information than in the past. Because corporations are more likely to support imaginative linkages between nonprofit organizations and the corporations' own business interests, industry information is critical.

Are there possibilities for other roles for the corporation beyond or in lieu of funding: in-kind support, hosting an event, board membership, meeting space, technical support, or employee volunteer opportunities?

Does the company have an employee matching gift program? HEP/CASE (http://case.hepdata.com) offers annual subscriptions to their GiftPlus OnLine service, which provides details on more than 15,000 matching gift companies.

Is this company a member of the chamber of commerce? Are there any ways you can collaborate with the company? The best way to answer this question is for your nonprofit institution to be a member of the chamber. This is one of the easiest ways for nonprofits to build bridges to the corporate community, establish long-term relationships, and take every opportunity to educate corporations about a societal need and about your approach to addressing it.

A company's grant making indicates its interest in leveraging corporate resources to give back to the community. Understandably, this is not a company's top priority. When a company uses resources that could readily be allocated for new equipment, product development, or the hiring of employees, a charitable gift must necessarily provide some element of recognition or benefit to the company. Corporate philanthropy balances altruism and self-interest. Nonprofits need to recognize these needs by explaining how they might work together with a company for mutual benefit and how the grant will be publicized in order to give the company favorable recognition in the communities of interest to it.

ASSOCIATIONS

Professional associations can also be a source of grants to public and other libraries. An Internet search under "association grants to libraries" can yield interesting results by identifying a number of associations and societies that have grant
programs, both of a permanent or an ad hoc nature. Of these associations, the
American Library Association offers the most opportunities for public libraries.
The ALA and its member units offer a variety of grants that provide funding or
material support for present or future activities. Grants may be offered to support
the planning and implementation of programs, to aid in the preparation of a
dissertation or other publications, and to promote research in library and information science. Grants are also given to support travel to conferences or other
events that can broaden an individual's experience or education in librarian-
ship. The ALA Awards Program, the ALA Scholarship Program, as well as ALA's
divisions, offices, round tables, and sections all administer grant programs.
For more information, visit the "grants" link on the ALA's website (www.ala
.org/ala/awardsgrants/grants/index.cfm).

Several special library-oriented associations offer grant and scholarship opportunities for individuals and funding for special projects. These include the Special
Libraries Association's Scholarship Program awards for graduate study and grants
for research projects and the Medical Library Association's scholarships and grants
to graduate library students and practicing health sciences librarians.

Two good education-oriented Internet resources which identify association
and other grant opportunities for librarians and library/information science students are the University of North Carolina's "Grants for Library Science Students" (http://research.unc.edu/grantsource/library_science.php) and Michigan
State University's "Grants for Individuals: Library and Information Science"
(http://staff.lib.msu.edu/harris23/grants/3libsci.htm). The scholarship opportunities listed by these sites cover a surprisingly diverse universe of associations and
businesses, including the American Antiquarian Society, American Association of
Law Libraries, American Association of University Women, Art Libraries Society
of North America, Association for Library and Information Science Education,
Association of Jewish Libraries, Beta Phi Mu, Bibliographical Society of Amer-
ica, Bibliographical Society (United Kingdom), California Library Association,
Chinese American Librarians Association, Council on Library and Information
Resources, Dialog Corporation, Maryland State Archives, Museum of Modern
Art, Music Library Association, North Carolina Library Association, North
Carolina School Library Media Association, and the Smithsonian Institution.

Occasionally, two grantors may team up to offer grants, such as a professional association and a foundation. For example, in January 2009 the International City/County Management Association (ICMA) introduced a Local Government and Public Libraries Initiative grant competition funded by a $500,000 gift from the Bill & Melinda Gates Foundation. The ICMA solicited joint proposals from local government/public library consortiums for projects demonstrating innovative approaches to using community libraries. The ICMA's individual Public Library Innovation Grants to cities, towns, and counties range from $25,000 to $75,000. This program is described at www.icma.org/public_libraries.

FEDERAL GOVERNMENT GRANT INFORMATION SOURCES

It is wise to consider all levels of government, including federal, state, and local, as potential sources of grants to public libraries. Over the last ten years, the U.S. government has responded to the needs of grant seekers by consolidating access to the multitude of federal opportunities in the form of a website known as Grants.gov, which is discussed below.

Grants.gov: The U.S. Federal Grants Website

There are many federal government agencies that offer grants to support research in science, technology, and medicine as well as to support education, the arts, and the humanities. The best and most comprehensive guide to federal government grants is Grants.gov (www.grants.gov). The charter of Grants.gov is to provide a unified electronic storefront for interactions between grant applicants and the federal agencies that manage grant funds. There are 26 federal grant-making agencies and more than 1,000 competitive grants programs that award a total of more than $400 billion in grants each year. You can sign up at the Grants.gov website to get automatic e-mail alerts about grant opportunities that are of interest to your organization. However, a recent *Washington Post* article reported that the government's 2009 stimulus program (the American Recovery and Reinvestment Act) was expected to increase grant activity by 60 percent, thereby severely taxing the ability of Grants.gov to keep up.[3] To manage the increasing number of federal grants, a major upgrade to the Grants.gov system was completed in February 2010. The upgrade increased the capacity of

Grants.gov, along with the system's reliability and its ability to sustain continuous high-volume activity. Moreover, there are alternative ways to access federal grant applications and information. Alternate routes include going to individual agency websites such as those of the Department of Energy, the Department of the Interior, or the Office of Community Oriented Policing Services at the Department of Justice, which have set up their own systems to accept applications.

In order to register in Grants.gov you must have a *DUNS number* (see below). If you have never registered in Grants.gov, the process can take up to two weeks to complete. In order to electronically apply for a federal grant through Grants .gov, you or your organization must complete the Central Contractor Registration (CCR) process. One can request registration for either organizational or individual grants. The normal registration process can take between three to five business days or as long as two weeks if the applying organization needs to obtain a mandatory Employer Identification Number (EIN) or DUNS number. The Grants Executive Board (GEB), which is the governing body of Grants. gov, has mandated the CCR registration process. The GEB has determined that this registration process needs to be completed prior to the submission of a grant application. Separate registrations for either an organization or an individual are required.

To register an organization with Grants.gov, these steps are required:

1. Register with Central Contractor Registration by phone (1-888-227-2423) or online (at www.ccr.gov) with instructions at (www .ccr.gov/handbook.asp).

2. Designate an organizational E-Business Point of Contact (E-Biz POC) and password (M-PIN).

3. The E-Biz POC may designate additional Authorized Organization Representatives (AORs) who are also eligible to submit electronic grant applications to Grants.gov from that organization.

Note that you will have to use Adobe Reader to attach required documents when you submit a federal grant application through Grants.gov.

You can also subscribe to receive notifications of new grant opportunity postings and updates on Grants.gov. You don't need to be a registered user of Grants.gov to sign up for this free service, which offers several levels of e-mail subscriptions:

Grants.gov RSS Feed (www.grants.gov/help/rss.jsp): new and updated grant opportunities

Grants.gov Updates (www.grants.gov/applicants/email_subscription_ signup.jsp): updated information about critical issues, new tips for users, and other time-sensitive updates as information is available

All Grants Notices (www.grants.gov/search/subscribeAll.do): daily notification of all new grant opportunities

Notices Based on Advanced Criteria (www.grants.gov/search/subscribe Advanced.do): select notifications based on specific criteria such as funding instrument type, eligibility, or sub-agency.

Number Notifications Based on Funding Opportunity Number (FON; www.grants.gov/search/email.do): a FON is a number that a federal agency assigns to each grant announcement

Catalog of Federal Domestic Assistance

The *Catalog of Federal Domestic Assistance* (CFDA; www.cfda.gov) lists all federal funding programs available to state and local governments (including the District of Columbia); federally recognized Indian tribal governments; territories and possessions of the United States; domestic public, quasi-public, and private profit and nonprofit organizations and institutions; specialized groups; and individuals. This tool, covering over 1,300 opportunities, is not as grant-specific as Grants.gov because in addition to federal formula and project grants, the *CFDA* also lists federal loans, insurance, sales of property and goods, counseling, and training and employment opportunities. After finding a desired program, one must then contact the office that administers the program and find out how to apply.

Federal Register

The *Federal Register* (www.gpoaccess.gov/fr/index.html) also lists federal grant opportunities. It is the official daily publication for rules, proposed rules, and notices of federal agencies and organizations, as well as executive orders and other presidential documents. It is updated daily by 6:00 a.m. and is published Monday through Friday. Search under "Notices of Funding Availability" or "Notices Inviting Applications."

FEDERAL GRANTS TO INDIVIDUALS

Although there are many grants on Grants.gov, few of them are available to individuals and none of them are available for personal financial aid. To find an alphabetical listing of federal grants and other programs for individuals, visit

the USA.gov website Government Benefits, Grants, and Financial Aid (www
.usa.gov/Citizen/Topics/Benefits.shtml). To find out if you are eligible to apply
for grants on Grants.gov, watch the helpful animated eligibility tutorial at www
.grants.gov/tutorials/gdgeligibility/Animated2009/index.htm.

If an individual submits a grant request on her own behalf and not on behalf of
a company, organization, institution, or government, she will only be able to apply
for grant opportunities that are open to individuals. An individual cannot submit
a grant application for a grant opportunity that is only open to organizations.

GROUPS ELIGIBLE FOR FEDERAL GRANTS

There are many types of organizations that are eligible to apply for government
grants. You can find out what grants are currently available in different eligibility categories by visiting the "Advanced Search" page on Grants.gov.

Typically, most grantee organizations fall into the following categories:

Government organizations

- state governments
- local governments
- city or township governments
- special district governments
- Native American tribal governments (federally recognized)
- Native American tribal governments (other than federally recognized)

Education organizations

- independent and government-controlled public libraries
- independent public school districts
- public and state-controlled institutions of higher education
- private institutions of higher education

Public housing organizations

- public housing authorities
- Native American housing authorities

Nonprofit organizations

- nonprofits having a 501(c)(3) status with the IRS, other than
  institutions of higher education

◆ nonprofits that do not have 501(c)(3) status with the IRS, other
than institutions of higher education

For-profit organizations

◆ although rare, grants (but more frequently loans) are occasionally
made to for-profit corporations for research and development
projects of interest to the government or as seed money to start
small businesses (see below)

Small businesses

◆ small business loans and small business grants may be awarded
to companies that meet the size standards that the U.S. Small
Business Administration (SBA) has established for most industries
in the economy. The most common small business upper-threshold
size limits are

500 employees for most manufacturing and mining industries

100 employees for all wholesale trade industries

$6 million for most retail and service industries

$28.5 million for most general and heavy construction industries

$12 million for all special trade contractors

$750,000 for most agricultural industries

Note that there are some exceptions to these standards, but virtually
all federal agencies and many state and local governments use these
size standards established by the SBA. You can search for further
information and for loan opportunities on the Small Business
Administration's website (www.sba.gov).

FEDERAL LIBRARY-ORIENTED GRANTING AGENCIES

For libraries, a major source of large federal grants (i.e., $10,000 or more) is
the U.S. Institute of Museum and Library Services (IMLS). Among its granting activities, IMLS funds the Grants to States program, which is also known
as the Library Services and Technology Act (LSTA) grants. LSTA grants are
usually distributed through state library agencies. A summary of the national
LSTA program can be viewed at www.imls.gov/pdf/CatalystForChange
.pdf. The IMLS also offers some individual library and museum grants, and

the IMLS Grant and Award Opportunities website is worth looking at (www .imls.gov/applicants/applicants.shtm). This site lists grant opportunities, giving deadlines, eligibility criteria, and proposal requirements. On occasion, state library agencies offer LSTA library education grants to individual public library staff members enrolled in university graduate library school programs. LSTA grants may also be used to fund local continuing education workshops for public librarians.

The following is a classified selection of major federal government agencies that have ongoing grant programs. Their granting activities can be viewed at Grants.gov (as discussed earlier in this chapter) or by going directly to each agency's website.

Arts, humanities, and education grants

Education—Department of Education

Humanities—National Endowment for the Humanities

Libraries and archives—National Archives and Records Administration

Museums—Institute of Museum and Library Services

Visual and performing arts—National Endowment for the Arts

Community and social services grants

Employment and labor—Department of Labor

Housing—Department of Housing and Urban Development

Law enforcement—Department of Justice

Health and medicine grants

Cancer research—National Cancer Institute

Health care services—Health Resources and Services Administration

Medicine—National Institutes of Health

Science, technology, and environment grants

Energy sciences—Department of Energy

Environmental grants and fellowships—Environmental Protection Agency

Natural resources—Fish and Wildlife Service

Scientific research—National Science Foundation

Small business research and development—Small Business Administration

> *Technology and engineering*—National Institute of Standards and Technology
>
> *Telecommunications*—National Telecommunications and Information Administration

Although the grant offerings of each of these federal agencies are listed in the umbrella Grants.gov website, each of these organizations also has its own website, with links to their grant activities. If you know which federal agencies you want to target in your grant seeking, you may be better advised to go directly to their websites and avoid the growing backlogs on Grants.gov which were being reported at the time of this writing.

PREREQUISITES TO FEDERAL GRANT SEEKING

If your organization is seeking grants (or loans) directly from the federal government, you must satisfy two basic prerequisites:

- ◆ Submission of the OMB Standard Form 424 (SF-424) Application for Federal Assistance, and supporting documents from the SF-424 family of forms
- ◆ Possession of an institutional DUNS number

These two items are explained below.

The SF-424 Family of Federal Forms

In partnership with federal grant-making agencies, Grants.gov has established the Standard Form 424 (SF-424) Form Families as the core government-wide standard data sets and forms for grant and loan application packages. Use of the SF-424 Form Families reduces the administrative burden to the federal grants community, which includes applicants, grantees, and federal staff involved in grants-related activities. The SF-424 Form Families include the following government-wide grant application cover sheets, forms, form data analysis templates, and form schema:

Standard Form	Individual Form
Research & Related Form	Key Contacts Form

Mandatory Form   Project Abstract Form

Short Organizational Form

The Standard Form SF-424 is illustrated in figure 4.1 and is available from government granting agencies and online at Grants.gov. Other federal grant forms are available from the Office of Management and Budget's website (www .whitehouse.gov/omb/grants/grants_forms.html). Note that some federal agencies may employ a slightly modified Form SF-424, but most will also accept the standard form. It is good practice, however, to verify with your government agency of interest which specific grant form is appropriate.

The DUNS Number

Since 2003, the federal government has required organizations applying to it for a grant, loan, or cooperative agreement to have a Data Universal Numbering System (DUNS) number. The DUNS number is a unique nine-character identification code provided at no charge by the commercial company Dun & Bradstreet. The DUNS number is also a prerequisite for registration in the federal government's Central Contractor Registry. Registration in this system is a requirement for all grantees applying for federal assistance through the federal Grants.gov website (www.grants.gov).

To obtain a DUNS number by telephone takes about ten minutes. To do so, call Dun & Bradstreet at 866-705-5711. Be prepared to answer the following questions:

a. Name of organization

b. Business address

c. Local phone number

d. Name of the CEO

e. Legal structure of the organization (e.g., corporation, partnership, proprietorship, etc.)

f. Year organization started

g. Primary line of organization (e.g., public library)

h. Total number of employees (full- and part-time)

You also may apply for a DUNS number online at the Dun & Bradstreet website: www.dnb.com/US/duns_update. The number will then be provided via e-mail within fourteen business days.

FIGURE 4.1

APPLICATION FOR FEDERAL ASSISTANCE, STANDARD FORM 424

OMB Number: 4040-0004
Expiration Date: 01/31/2009

Application for Federal Assistance SF-424	Version 02

* 1. Type of Submission:
☐ Preapplication
☐ Application
☐ Changed/Corrected Application

* 2. Type of Application:
☐ New
☐ Continuation
☐ Revision

* If Revision, select appropriate letter(s):
[_____]

* Other (Specify):
[_____]

* 3. Date Received:
Completed by Grants.gov upon submission.

4. Applicant Identifier:

5a. Federal Entity Identifier:

* 5b. Federal Award Identifier:

State Use Only:

6. Date Received by State:

7. State Application Identifier:

8. APPLICANT INFORMATION:

* a. Legal Name:

* b. Employer/Taxpayer Identification Number (EIN/TIN):

* c. Organizational DUNS:

d. Address:

* Street1:
Street2:
* City:
County:
* State:
Province:
* Country: USA: UNITED STATES
* Zip / Postal Code:

e. Organizational Unit:

Department Name:

Division Name:

f. Name and contact information of person to be contacted on matters involving this application:

Prefix:
* First Name:
Middle Name:
* Last Name:
Suffix:

Title:

Organizational Affiliation:

* Telephone Number:

Fax Number:

* Email:

OMB Number: 4040-0004
Expiration Date: 01/31/2009

Application for Federal Assistance SF-424	Version 02

9. Type of Applicant 1: Select Applicant Type:

Type of Applicant 2: Select Applicant Type:

Type of Applicant 3: Select Applicant Type:

* Other (specify):

* 10. Name of Federal Agency:

NGMS Agency

11. Catalog of Federal Domestic Assistance Number:

CFDA Title:

* 12. Funding Opportunity Number:

MBL-SF424FAMILY-ALLFORMS

* Title:

MBL-SF424Family-AllForms

13. Competition Identification Number:

Title:

14. Areas Affected by Project (Cities, Counties, States, etc.):

* 15. Descriptive Title of Applicant's Project:

Attach supporting documents as specified in agency instructions.

Add Attachments   Delete Attachments   View Attachments

(cont.)

41

FIGURE 4.1 APPLICATION FOR FEDERAL ASSISTANCE, STANDARD FORM 424 (cont.)

Expiration Date: 01/31/2009

Application for Federal Assistance SF-424	Version 02

16. Congressional Districts Of:

* a. Applicant   * b. Program/Project

Attach an additional list of Program/Project Congressional Districts if needed.

Add Attachment   Delete Attachment   View Attachment

17. Proposed Project:

* a. Start Date: * b. End Date:

18. Estimated Funding ($):

* a. Federal

* b. Applicant

* c. State

* d. Local

* e. Other

* f. Program Income

* g. TOTAL

* 19. Is Application Subject to Review By State Under Executive Order 12372 Process?

☐ a. This application was made available to the State under the Executive Order 12372 Process for review on

☐ b. Program is subject to E.O. 12372 but has not been selected by the State for review.

☐ c. Program is not covered by E.O. 12372.

* 20. Is the Applicant Delinquent On Any Federal Debt? (If "Yes", provide explanation.)

☐ Yes   ☐ No   Explanation

21. *By signing this application, I certify (1) to the statements contained in the list of certifications** and (2) that the statements herein are true, complete and accurate to the best of my knowledge. I also provide the required assurances** and agree to comply with any resulting terms if I accept an award. I am aware that any false, fictitious, or fraudulent statements or claims may subject me to criminal, civil, or administrative penalties. (U.S. Code, Title 218, Section 1001)

☐ **** I AGREE**

** The list of certifications and assurances, or an internet site where you may obtain this list, is contained in the announcement or agency specific instructions.

Authorized Representative:

Prefix: * First Name:

Middle Name:

* Last Name:

Suffix:

* Title:

* Telephone Number: Fax Number:

* Email:

* Signature of Authorized Representative: Completed by Grants.gov upon submission.   * Date Signed: Completed by Grants.gov upon submission.

Authorized for Local Reproduction

Standard Form 424 (Revised 10/2005)
Prescribed by OMB Circular A-102

| Application for Federal Assistance SF-424 | Version 02 |

* Applicant Federal Debt Delinquency Explanation

The following field should contain an explanation if the Applicant organization is delinquent on any Federal Debt. Maximum number of characters that can be entered is 4,000. Try and avoid extra spaces and carriage returns to maximize the availability of space.

GOVERNMENT PERFORMANCE
AND RESULTS ACT OF 1993

Not-for-profit federal grant seekers should be aware of the Government Performance and Results Act of 1993, often called GPRA, or simply the Results Act. Though not usually a mandatory datum requirement for a federal grant (such as the DUNS number), the Results Act requires federal agencies to develop strategic plans, performance measures, annual performance plans, and performance reporting tied to their budgets. It is cited in most federal grant RFPs, and for some agencies, applicants or grantees may be required to state how their grant project supports the granting agency's GPRA (i.e., how they will use resources wisely in achieving program results within the funding agency's mission and budget). The GPRA requires strategic planning efforts to include several linked activities:

- planning, to achieve goals and objectives
- budgeting, to ensure that resources are available to carry out plans
- measuring, to assess progress and link resources actually used to the results achieved
- reporting, to present progress achieved and impacts on future efforts

Regardless of the GPRA, these are all elements that should be included in a well-run grant project (in addition to a well-written grant proposal). Therefore, by specifically citing and including these tasks (i.e., planning, budgeting, measuring, and reporting) and how they relate to your goal in your federal grant proposal and reports, you will help the funding federal agency in both its budgetary justification and program results evaluation. This can only strengthen your position as a prospective and actual grantee.

To learn more about the GPRA, go to the OMB's website at www .whitehouse.gov/omb/mgmt-gpra/gplaw2m.html.

ARRA (STIMULUS) FEDERAL AND STATE FUNDS

On February 16, 2009, President Obama signed the American Recovery and Reinvestment Act (ARRA), commonly known as the "stimulus package," into law. Since then, many federal agencies have established their own Recovery Act web pages, which include weekly reports containing information on funding, major actions taken so far, and those actions planned for the near term. These websites can guide grant seekers to funding programs for which they may be eligible. The central ARRA website is www.recovery.gov/?q=content/agencies.

At the time of this writing, several federal agencies of interest to libraries maintain ARRA information websites: the Agency for International Development, Corporation for National and Community Service, Department of Agriculture, Department of Commerce, Department of Defense, Department of Education, Department of Energy, Department of Health and Human Services, Department of Housing and Urban Development, Department of the Interior, Department of Transportation, Environmental Protection Agency, National Endowment for the Arts, National Science Foundation, Small Business Administration, Smithsonian Institution, and the Social Security Administration, among others. The word on the street among grant writers is that the government's vision in making ARRA grants is to create jobs, spend quickly and efficiently with transparency and accountability, and to stimulate the economy with supplemental funding. Therefore, show that your proposal will fulfill this vision and collaborate with a partner in an ARRA application!

A valuable link at the ARRA website is "State Progress and Resources," which gives access to state websites providing information on the stimulus funds available within each state, such as http://recovery.alabama.gov, www.recovery.pa.gov, www.recovery.vermont.gov, and so on.

PREVAILING WAGE RULES ON FEDERALLY FUNDED GRANTS (DAVIS-BACON AND RELATED ACTS)

If federal grant or loan monies are being employed on a construction project, the prevailing wage rules of Davis-Bacon and Related Acts (DBRA) will most likely apply. The DBRA requires all contractors and subcontractors performing work on federal and District of Columbia construction or federally assisted contracts in excess of $2,000 to pay their laborers and mechanics not less than the prevailing wage rates and fringe benefits for corresponding classes of laborers and mechanics employed on similar projects in the area. The secretary of labor determines the prevailing wage rates and fringe benefits for covered government contracts. You can find more information on the DBRA at www.dol.gov/compliance/laws/comp-dbra.htm. Note that many states also require prevailing wages be paid on state grant-funded construction projects. Listings of DBRA prevailing wage rates by state and county can be found at www.gpo.gov/davisbacon/allstates.html.

STATE GOVERNMENT

In my library's experience, state government has been the primary source of public library grant money, both for state funds and as a distribution channel for federal grant dollars. This is due largely to the annual cycle of LSTA grants (up to $100,000 each in some states) by which state libraries distribute federal IMLS funds to public libraries, museums, and schools. Some states also earmark monies generated from specific taxes (such as that on athletes and entertainers in Missouri, realty transfers in Pennsylvania, and license plate fees in Texas) to fund library grant competitions that can offer construction grants for up to $500,000 per project. There are other state grants, some recurring annually, which fund a variety of library projects such as energy conservation, services to special groups, and preservation. Some states, such as Illinois and Missouri, offer "equalization grants" to help public libraries that have a low local tax base achieve a minimum level of funding for local library services. I have learned that the best way to find out about state public library grant opportunities is through your state library. Access your state library's website and click or search under "grants" to find out what is available in your state. An example of a particularly well-organized and informative state guide to available public library grants is found on the Texas State Library and Archives Commission's website: www.tsl.state.tx.us/ld/funding.

Developing a relationship with your state library's district consultant or county liaison person can also be helpful. Ask her to apprise and advise you of relevant grant opportunities. These individuals are usually quite approachable and helpful and can provide administrative and technical advice on putting a grant proposal together. When my state library switched from hard copy to electronic submission of LSTA grant proposals, my library district consultant helped me to master the confusing new world of online proposal submission. Advice on online proposal submission can be found in chapter 11.

You can also contact your state legislators and ask them if they can assist you in obtaining state grant funds. They may be aware of community development, conservation, or discretionary legislative grant funds that your institution is eligible to apply for. A helpful legislator may even ask his legislative assistant to do a little investigative legwork for you as my state senator did for me. Some states provide discretionary grant funds to legislators for them to disburse within their districts. For example, in my home state of Pennsylvania, a state fund of over $100 million is annually divided up among legislators to distribute as Community Revitalization Program grants for projects in their constituencies. Many Pennsylvania public libraries (including my own) have requested and received these grants (popularly known as Walking Around Money, or "WAM grants") for amounts of $5,000 or more.

COUNTY AND LOCAL GOVERNMENT

It is wise to consult with the financial people at your county and municipal government agencies to determine if they have any grant monies available to public libraries. County redevelopment authorities and large metropolitan and urban areas have been known to develop grant programs similar to those usually found at the state level, which may be of benefit to public libraries.

NOTES

1. Deborah Ward, ed., *Writing Grant Proposals That Win* (Sudbury, MA: Jones and Bartlett, 2006), 58.

2. Bernie Jankowski, "5 Things to Find Out about a Potential Corporate Sponsor," *Nonprofit Times*, NPT Instant Fundraising, May 5, 2009, http://ga0.org/nptimes/join.html.

3. *Washington Post*, "Grants.gov Strains Under New Demand," March 12, 2009, A17.

Initiating Contact
with Grantors

Employing the institutional self-analysis recommended in the prior chapters, it is assumed that by now your library will have determined that grantsmanship is something you want to pursue, and you know the reasons why and what for. With this ammunition in your hunter's pack, you will be ready to find and approach a potential donor.

In selecting a grantor and defining a project opportunity to pursue, keep in mind that scheduling your campaign is important because most foundations and granting agencies operate on prescribed annual or even biennial grant cycles. If you miss a cycle, you might have to wait a while for the next round to begin.

EMPLOYING A GRANTOR ANALYSIS WORKSHEET

As you begin to evaluate potential grantors, you will find that matching your grant need with a prospective grantor is really a form of market analysis as a prelude to the "sale," which is the winning of your grant. Your organization will be "selling" its need, qualifications, and project plan to the grantor via a proposal. However, as with all selling, your "advertising" and "sales pitch" is always more effective if you understand your client. Therefore, it is advisable to collect and analyze relevant information on the prospective grantors you are considering. To facilitate the gathering and evaluation of information on grantors you identify, you can employ a prospect worksheet such as the two suggested by the Foundation Center and shown in appendix A as figures A.1 and A.2. Figure A.1 shows the Prospect Worksheet for Institutional Funders and figure A.2 shows the one for Individual Donors. Note that the Institutional Funder Worksheet lists sources for obtaining this background information such as IRS Form 990-PF and annual reports, as well as directories and the grant maker's website.

PRE-PROPOSAL MARKETING CONTACT WITH PROSPECTIVE GRANTORS

Once you have identified one or more prospective grantors, you have two general approaches, proactive or reactive. Which one you choose will largely be determined by the policy and procedure of the grantor you are pursuing. You can be proactive if, for example, the grantor is a small private foundation or individual without a prescribed granting procedure and schedule. Here, you may initiate contact leading to submission of an unsolicited proposal. However, if the grantor is a government agency or a large foundation, they will most likely eschew unsolicited proposals in favor of issuing competitive solicitations (i.e., RFPs). Then you go into reactive mode, monitoring the grantor's activity and waiting until they issue an RFP to which you can then respond.

There are varying views on the level of pre-proposal marketing contact one should have with a grantor organization. Some grantors may encourage this, some may tolerate it, and some may discourage it. Check the grantor's literature and website to determine their communication guidelines, and follow their rules. If telephone calls or visits seem appropriate, then contact the grantor and explain your institution's situation and needs and ask if their grants program might be relevant and what application procedures must be followed. Do your homework and be organized, concise, and specific in your descriptions and queries. Granting officers often have to deal with scores of prospective grantees and they appreciate a direct approach. You may benefit from this contact by establishing a personal rapport, getting good advice regarding future grant requests, and, perhaps, softly pre-selling your institution and its proposed project. However, if the grantor discourages advance personal contact or limits it to only letters or e-mails and only on specific questions, then follow their guidance rather than running the risk of creating the negative impression that your organization does not respect their rules. You want the grantor to look forward to receiving your proposal, not dread further contact with you, so remember my grant rule number 8: *Do not be a pest!*

UNSOLICITED NONCOMPETITIVE APPROACHES

An important point to remember is that grantors do not like surprises. Therefore, never submit an unsolicited proposal to an organization or individual donor until you have ascertained that they are amenable to receiving and considering it for funding. This can often be done somewhat informally by making an appointment for an exploratory visit, if the potential grantor is nearby, or via an exploratory letter of inquiry, telephone call, or e-mail. Some grantor agencies, however, may require formal letters of inquiry or letters of interest (also known as a letter of intent, or LOI for short). The following sections cover LOIs in more detail.

LETTERS OF INTENT, INQUIRY, OR INTEREST

Reduced grant funding and the submission of naive, ineligible, or frivolous grant applications by some wannabe grantees have caused some grantors to prescreen prospective grantees. This is done by requiring that they first submit a "letter of inquiry," also known as a "letter of interest," or the somewhat different "letter of intent" before receiving either an RFP or the grantor's permission to submit a proposal. All these prescreen submissions are generally known as LOIs. LOI requirements vary by grantor and can range from a simple one-page expression of intent to a two- or three-page proposal in microcosm. A discussion of LOI content and format follows, and sample LOIs can be found in figures 5.1 and 5.2.

In introducing these first two formal grant submission documents, I will also introduce a hard rule that should govern your entire grant proposal-writing activity as my rule number 6: *Read the grantor's instructions and give them exactly what they want!*

Whether you are preparing a one-page letter of intent or a hundred-page proposal, you must religiously adhere to the instructions provided by the grantor. Include everything they ask for and add nothing that they do not want. Follow the format they specify. Failure to follow instructions precisely will create a negative impression, and the grantor will not look forward to working with you or your organization. Grant reviewers receive many submissions, and you will make their work easier by providing the consistent format they need to be able to compare and evaluate. They will appreciate it.

Letters of Intent

Some grant-writing mentors make no distinction between the letter of intent and the letter of inquiry. An exception is Burke Smith, who explains that letters of intent are for reactive grant seeking and are used to advise a grantor that a proposal will be forthcoming in response to an RFP.[1] In contrast, letters of inquiry are really mini-proposals required by grantors to prequalify prospective grantees before they are invited to submit a full proposal. The letter of intent may be requested by a foundation or government agency to determine how many grant proposals it is likely to receive in response to an RFP. The letter of intent is usually not used to determine eligibility to apply. Letters of intent should be brief and simple and should be confined to a single page unless the grantor requests more information. They should be sent to the specified grantor contact, specify the name and ID of the grant opportunity, and should be signed by the grantee's CEO or board chair. Some granting agencies may provide a letter of intent application form, such as the example shown in figure 5.1 for a state library construction grant. This letter of intent is interesting because the state requires that it be jointly submitted by both the public library requesting the grant and the municipality in which the library resides, and that at least one of the prospective grantees must certify their prior attendance at a pre-proposal workshop. When using any proposal or pre-proposal form such as this, make sure that you are employing the latest version. Forms do evolve over time, and grant forms may change from year to year. Using an outdated form can cost you review points with the grantor and may cause you to omit required information.

In the letter of intent, remind the RFP issuer that you are interested in being kept informed about any modification related to the project solicitation (i.e., the RFP document). A letter of intent is not, by essence, a binding document, and if your circumstances or interests change, you may withdraw you intention to respond to an RFP. It is best to do this by a formal withdrawal letter to the recipient of the original letter of intent.

Letters of Inquiry/Interest

A letter of inquiry (also known as a letter of interest) allows a grantor to prescreen potential candidates for funding, making sure that the grantor does not

FIGURE 5.1

SAMPLE STATE LETTER OF INTENT FORM

LETTER OF INTENT to apply for Recreation, Park, and Conservation Fund Grant Program for Public Library Facilities

This Letter of Intent is **due** at the State Library on **January 30, 2009.**

This **Letter of Intent** has been completed to inform the State Library that the municipality of _____ plans to apply for a grant in the
NAME OF MUNICIPALITY

amount of _____ for the benefit of _____
REQUEST NAME OF PUBLIC LIBRARY

The estimated cost of the total project: _____

Estimated new square footage: _____

The proposed project summary: _____

_____

_____

_____

_____

Estimated time needed for project: _____ **months**

It is understood that a municipal or library representative, who will be completing the application, *must* have attended a State Library grant workshop or webinar during this current round in order to proceed with an application.*

Name of attendee: _____ Title: _____

Date Attended:_____

It is understood that a subsequent receipt of an "Invitation to Proceed with Application" from the State Library does not guarantee that the project will be funded.

_____

*If an outside grant writer is responsible for the application, the grant writer as well as a municipal or library representative, who will be responsible for implementing the project, *must* have also attended. Please include name and title of additional attendees, and date of attendance, on the back of this page.

Both the municipality, public library, and District Consultant Librarian are aware of the intention of submitting an application and, if the library is part of a System, the Library System Board has approved the project:

Municipality Contact

Name:

Address:

E-mail address:

Library Contact

Name:

Address:

E-mail address:

_____   _____
SIGNATURE   DATE   SIGNATURE   DATE

Date of Historical Site Clearance Review: _____

System Board Official Name: _____

Address:_____

E-mail address: _____

Name of District Consultant: _____

Signature: _____Date:_____

Date Consultant was notified: _____

waste its time on evaluating a full proposal for an inappropriate project that does not fit with its mission or budget. For the grant seeker, the LOI is a proposal in microcosm and a marketing tool that allows you to pre-sell your project and your qualifications in order to receive an invitation to submit a complete proposal. Generally, a cold LOI (i.e., no prior contact between prospective grantor and grantee) is not recommended unless the grantor has advertised that this is an acceptable practice. Always contact the grant organization first and ask about their procedures for allowing prospective grantees to request grants. They will tell you if an LOI is required as a pre-proposal condition.

The LOI is really a marketing tool, which should whet the appetite of the grantor and make them ask for more. Again, as with all grant-seeking activities, honor rule number 6: *Read the grantor's instructions and give them exactly what they want!*

Letter of Inquiry/Interest Content

If LOI instructions are absent or not specific, then you can follow these suggested format guidelines and the format shown in figure 5.2, which presents a sample letter of inquiry.

LOI size: A typical letter-format LOI is up to three pages long, plus a one-page budget addendum if required.

Letterhead: Use a formal letterhead, and do not handwrite the letter of intent.

Heading: Type "Letter of Inquiry" or Letter of Intent" at the top of your letter or in the "Subject" line (see below).

Subject line: State the purpose of the LOI (e.g., "Letter of Inquiry for ABC Project Grant"). It can be useful to develop a concise and interesting project title to use here (e.g., "The Main Street Library Outpost").

Introductory paragraph: First, indicate your interest in receiving a grant and acknowledge any deadlines for the proposal you will submit. Include a concise "executive summary" that defines and qualifies your organization, describes the project, and contains a statement of project need and outcomes, the project timetable, and the needed funding. It is important to state here how the prospective project relates to the grantor's mission.

Organizational description and qualifications: Provide a concise summary of those aspects of your institution's mission, history, structure, constituency, qualifications, and programs which support the need for your proposed project and your ability to successfully complete it. Briefly cite any

FIGURE 5.2

SAMPLE LETTER OF INQUIRY

Bibliophile Memorial Public Library
24 River Road
Farmadelphia, PA 00000

October 1, 20XX

Mr. George G. Grantor, Administrator
Living Library Foundation
1 Main Street
Philanthropyberg, PA, XXXXX

SUBJECT: Letter of Inquiry: Grant Request for Computer Instruction
for Technologically Handicapped Senior Citizens under Your Rural Public
Library Technology Grant Program

REFERENCE: Our Meeting of September 25th at Your Offices

Dear Mr. Grantor:

Thank you for allowing me to meet with you and your staff at the Living Library
Foundation headquarters on September 25th. I thoroughly enjoyed my visit with
you and your staff. In particular, I appreciate the information and guidance you
shared with me regarding the Living Library Foundation's Rural Public Library
Technology Grant Program. Based on these discussions and analysis of the
documentation you provided, I believe that our library may be eligible for a
grant to provide a program of computer instruction to our area's technologically
handicapped seniors. We therefore express our interest in applying for a grant
under this program to offer a series of computer and Internet technology courses
specifically designed for seniors over a one-year period. Seniors are a priority user
group for our rural library, and the proposed program would build upon the basic
(and very popular) introductory computer classes we have offered at the library for
the past two years.

The Bibliophile Memorial Public Library was built and opened in 1999 thanks
to a bequest from the estate of Beatrice Bibliophile, a local philanthropist. Since
its opening, the population of the library's Farmadelphia service area has grown
from about 8,800 people to nearly 12,000. Many of the area's new residents are
retired senior citizens attracted by the area's quality of life and relatively low cost of
living. As a result, library use has increased at a compound growth rate of 20% per
year, with patron visits now approaching 60,000 per year and circulation of library
materials nearing 100,000 items annually. Because of the rural and somewhat
isolated nature of the library's Farmville service area, there is virtually no local social
services infrastructure and no nonsectarian community or learning centers beyond
the public schools. Therefore, by necessity, the library has become the focal
point for community information assistance, referral, learning, and recreational
activity. The Bibliophile Memorial Public Library has received two AARP Awards

of Excellence for Library Services to Seniors and has won several competitive government and foundation grants. The library is only partially supported by government funding and a modest endowment from Beatrice Bibliophile and must raise 45% of its operating budget from local fund drives and benefit events. There are no library funds available to provide instruction or library materials to satisfy the specific needs of special populations, and grants are the only means of acquiring funds for these needed programs.

Based on its assessment of Farmville community needs, the library has assigned priority status to those user groups whose learning and information cannot be satisfied by any other community agencies. As a result, seniors have been designated as high-priority populations. Local surveys have shown that senior citizens comprise over 30% of the area's population, and at least 50% of this group do not own home computers and/or have no or only a very rudimentary understanding of computer and Internet technology. Senior citizens need both the ability and tools to allow them to employ computers and the Internet to obtain necessary information, improve their quality of life, and allow their fixed incomes to go further. Many of these people now come to the library to request basic instruction on how to employ the Bibliophile Memorial Public Library's five public-access online computers to obtain necessary information on government programs such as Social Security and Medicare, establish referrals to county and state social services agencies, or purchase needed goods and services. The library is not equipped to provide individual computer instruction, but in response to demand it has been offering a basic introductory computer course for seniors, employing a volunteer instructor and five donated secondhand computers. This project has received favorable media coverage ("Bibliophile Library Enables Seniors to Get Wired," *Farmadelphia Reporter,* 1A, May 26, 20XX) and has attracted many new enrollees. As a result, the demand for basic instruction has exceeded library resources and has generated further requests for additional advanced computer instruction on such topics as e-mail, the Internet, MS Word, file management and storage media, computer graphics, and electronic publishing. To respond to this growing and important need in its senior citizen community, the Bibliophile Memorial Public Library desires to present a grant proposal to the Living Library Foundation to obtain funds to implement a computer instructional program for the technologically handicapped seniors in its service area.

The proposed grant project will begin by surveying the Farmadelphia area senior community to expand existing data already in hand on the computer learning needs of this population segment. These data will be used to develop a syllabus of approximately ten to fifteen computer instruction courses to be offered throughout the year at the library, including:

- Introduction to Computers;
- Introduction to MS Word and Office Suite;
- Sending and Receiving E-Mail;
- Surfing the Internet;
- Electronic Publishing;
- Websites of Interest to Seniors;

- Computer Graphics and Digital Cameras;
- Buying and Selling on the Internet;
- Computer File Management and Storage Media;
- Computer-Based Presentations (e.g., PowerPoint);
- Computer Security;
- Social Networking;
- etc.

Courses will be taught in two-hour sessions and range from four to ten hours total duration each and will be free to library cardholders.

Both volunteer and compensated instructors will be recruited from the area's professional and educational communities. Library administration will work with instructors to develop senior-friendly course content, duration, and scheduling. Course texts will be developed and/or acquired (e.g., the text series published by Web Wise Seniors). To supplement the library's existing complement of data processors, five desktop and five notebook instructional computers (Dell or equivalent) will be acquired for use by students both in the library classroom and as loaners to facilitate homework.

It is expected that this program will be able to train up to 500 senior students per year. Employing an outcome-based evaluation technique, students will be first surveyed at the initiation of each course cycle to determine their entry-level abilities and course expectations. A follow-up survey will also be conducted at course conclusion to determine if the instruction met the students' expectations and the extent to which computer skills were improved. Instructors will also be surveyed on their expectations for and evaluation of the courses.

Bibliophile Memorial Public Library's Assistant Director Deborah Decimal will directly supervise this project. She is in charge of all library educational programs and data processing efforts. Library Executive Director Seymour Shelflist will provide project oversight and reporting to the Foundation. Mr. Shelflist and Ms. Decimal will recruit both volunteer and paid instructors from among data processing professionals and high school and university educators in the Farmadelphia area. We plan to obtain the lion's share of instructors by partnering with Farmadelphia Junior College's Computer Science Department chaired by Dr. Boris Byte. Some courses (such as Surfing the Internet) will be taught by library reference staff. The library will publicize the availability of the instruction via press releases to the media, leaflet handouts, the library's newsletter and website, and posters in the library and displayed at public places throughout the community. The grant-funded development phase of the project will be twelve months where 10–15 courses will be designed and presented. Each course will be repeated at least twice, for at least 250 hours of classroom instruction. After the first year, the courses will be sustained with library-generated funding. During the grant period the Library will provide the Foundation with quarterly progress reports, with the final report being a complete project summary, including student evaluation data.

The total cost for the Computer Instruction for Technologically Handicapped Senior Citizens project is estimated at $50,000. The Bibliophile Memorial Public Library will cover $10,000 of the project costs with a grant from the Friends of the

Library and will require an additional grant of $40,000 from the Foundation to cover these necessary expenses:

1. Computer Instructional Labor: $20,000;
2. Computer Hardware: $15,000;
3. Textbooks and Instructional Materials: $5,000.

We thank the Living Library Foundation for the opportunity to submit this letter of inquiry to you. We sincerely hope that you will find the proposed project to provide Computer Instruction for Technologically Handicapped Senior Citizens to be worthy of your consideration for a grant and allow us to submit a full proposal to you. If you have any questions or require any additional information, please do not hesitate to contact Bibliophile Memorial Public Library Executive Director Seymour Shelflist at 717-000-0000 or shelflist@bibliophile.org, should you require any additional information.

Sincerely,

Timothea Trustee
Board President
Bibliophile Memorial Public Library

Attachments:
- Audited financial statement for the fiscal year ending December 31, 20XX
- IRS 501(c)(3) determination letter
- 20XX annual report

relevant awards and recognition. Here you must convince them that you have the smarts and resources to successfully do the job.

Statement of need/problem: It is essential that you convince the reader that there is a critical need or problem that the proposed project can fulfill and solve. Define the category of your project in terms of service to the community (e.g., youth education, service to homebound seniors, etc.). Cite the target population(s) and geographical area(s) with reference to supporting data (save detailed statistics for the full proposal). A strong quotation from an authoritative source can be included if available. If the project is unique, emphasize the features that make it so.

Project methodology: Logically outline the sequence of project tasks leading to the solution of the problem defined in your statement of need.

Project outcomes: State the expected results of the project (i.e., solutions to the stated needs) and their impact on target populations. Indicate that outcomes-based evaluation will be part of the project.

Management approach: State how the project will be organized, who will supervise and staff it, the project schedule, and the project "deliverables" (reports to grantor agency, events, publications, etc.). If you intend to partner with another organization, identify them here and their role. Refer to and include partnership letters of agreement as attachments.

Statement of costs (budget abstract): Provide a summary statement of total project cost, indicating the amount of the grant request as well as other sources of funding (including grantee matching funds and in-kind funding). Unless otherwise instructed, this summary budget should define costs in generic categories (e.g., labor, travel, library materials, etc.) and should not exceed one page. It is usually acceptable to round off here to the nearest hundred dollars (for small grants) or thousand dollars (for larger grants).

Closing statement: Offer here to provide any additional information or answer any questions as required by the grantor. Identify your organization's point of contact along with her telephone and e-mail. Express your appreciation for the grantor's attention and the opportunity to submit the LOI. Clearly request permission to submit a full proposal. If the grantor did not provide a timetable for their response, indicate that you will follow up in two weeks. Be sure to provide correct, complete contact and reference information for future correspondence.

Signature: To confirm institutional support for the grant request, have either your board president or the library director sign the LOI even if they are not the specified contact person. Finally, close the letter formally with "sincerely" or a similar polite expression. Sign your name and title.

Delivery: Send the letter of intent via a trackable delivery method (e.g., U.S. Postal Service Certified Mail with return receipt requested, USPS Registered Mail, USPS Priority Mail with delivery confirmation, USPS Priority Mail with signature confirmation, USPS Express Mail, etc.) or hand-deliver it if the grantor is local. Always ask for a receipt or confirmation of delivery.

COMMON GRANT APPLICATIONS

Certain groups of grantors have adopted a common grant application format to allow grant applicants to produce a single proposal for one or more members of a specific community of funders, thereby saving time. Common grant applications are most often used for unsolicited grant requests. Before applying to any funder that accepts a common grant application form, be sure to check that your project matches the funder's stated interests and ascertain whether the funder would prefer a letter of inquiry in advance of receiving a proposal. Also be sure to check whether the funder has a deadline for proposals, as well as whether it requires multiple copies of your proposal.

A typical common grant application such as the Minnesota Common Grant Application Form (www.mcf.org) consists of four components:

- ◆ Cover sheet, which asks for basic information about a grant seeker's organization and grant request
- ◆ Proposal narrative, which provides a detailed outline of the information that should be provided in a grant application
- ◆ Standard format for presenting an organization budget
- ◆ Standard format for presenting a project budget

Examples of common grant application groups in the United States are

- ◆ Association of Baltimore Area Grantmakers
- ◆ Colorado Common Grant Application
- ◆ Connecticut Council for Philanthropy
- ◆ Council of Michigan Foundations
- ◆ Donors Forum of Chicago
- ◆ Donors Forum of Wisconsin
- ◆ Grantmakers of Western Pennsylvania
- ◆ Maine Philanthropy Center
- ◆ Minnesota Common Grant Application Form
- ◆ New York/New Jersey Area Common Application Form
- ◆ Ohio Common Grant Forms
- ◆ Philanthropy Northwest (Alaska, Idaho, Montana, Oregon, and Washington)
- ◆ Washington Regional Association of Grantmakers

SUBMITTING THE SAME PROPOSAL TO MORE THAN ONE PROSPECTIVE GRANTOR

Some grant seekers may attempt to hedge their bets by submitting the same unsolicited grant request to more than one prospective granting agency. If you decide to do this, I recommend total honesty by advising each recipient of your request that it has been sent to other grantors. This may slightly lessen the chances of your award, because you may be perceived as just "shopping around," but your candor will, in turn, win you some points. If you submit a proposal to multiple funders and receive one or more awards as a result, you are ethically bound to notify and provide this information to the grantors and reviewers still considering your proposal(s).

There are, however, situations where a prospective grantee legitimately seeks joint partnership funding from more than one donor for a project. This can be the case where both the government and a foundation jointly fund a project or one partner may donate cash and another resources in-kind. Coordination among donors is important in cases like this.

NOTE

1. Nancy Burke Smith and E. Gabriel Works, *The Complete Book of Grant Writing* (Naperville, IL: Sourcebooks, 2006), 15.

Obtaining Solicited Competitive Grant Application Packages

By skillfully employing the grant and grantor information resources and tools described in chapter 4, you will be able to identify which organizations award grants in your areas of interest and will learn how to obtain requests for proposals for their grant competitions. The next step, therefore, is to obtain the RFPs you are interested in receiving, reviewing, and bidding upon. Obtaining an RFP from a grantor may be as simple as downloading it from the grantor's website or sending in a letter or e-mail to request a copy. However, in some cases the grantor may require preliminary screening or prequalification of prospective applicants before issuing them an RFP. These circumstances were outlined in chapter 5 and often include advance submission of a letter of inquiry, letter of intent, or attendance at a pre-proposal workshop.

Ask your prospective grantors if they require a common or standard application form. Certain granting organizations share common grant application forms, such as the federal government's Application for Federal Assistance (SF-424) described in chapter 4 and shown in figure 4.1, or the common grant application forms employed by several regional groups of foundations (see chapter 5). You may need to either complete one of the common forms in order to receive an RFP or you may have to submit the form as part of or in lieu of a proposal. Make sure you use the latest edition of these forms because they are regularly revised, and using an out-of-date form can lose you proposal points or even disqualify you.

STUDYING AND ANALYZING THE
GRANT SOLICITATION

Once you have received a grant solicitation package (RFP), it is important to take the time to carefully study it to determine:

a. Is this an appropriate grant opportunity for your institution to pursue? (See criteria in chapters 3 and 4.)

b. Will you be able to meet the RFP-mandated proposal deadline?

c. What strategies and resources will you need to employ in your proposal preparation?

d. How will you likely be rated on the RFP's stated evaluation criteria? (See also chapters 7 and 8.)

Preliminary answers to these questions will help you and your institution decide if this is a grant opportunity worth pursuing.

If your institution requires the approval of its governing or reviewing body prior to the pursuit of a grant, then this approval to proceed is also a step to include in your review and evaluation of the RFP.

Invest sufficient time in studying the granting agency's grant solicitation documents and particularly the rules for eligibility, criteria for awards, schedules and deadlines, funding limits, and any grantor missions and goals that pertain to their grant activities. In grant writing, treat the request for proposal as your Bible and Ten Commandments and follow its instructions religiously. Highlight what appear to be the principal foci of the grantor organization as stated in its documentation. Underline what seem to be buzzwords and phrases that are important to the grantor organization. Determine which action verbs are used with frequency in the documents. What you are doing here is identifying the focus of the organization's grant giving and what hot-button topics should be addressed in your application in order to demonstrate your mutual commitment to the same ideals. Put aside your pride of authorship and write your proposal using the section and paragraph headings, words, and style of the granting agency's literature and RFP. Your grant proposal's vocabulary will then be comfortably familiar and understandable to the grant evaluators because you are using their language. In the grantsmanship game, familiarity between grantor and grantee, rather than breeding contempt, facilitates award. Granting agencies tend to make awards to organizations that demonstrate similar missions, understanding, and values.

MAKING THE GO/NO-GO PROPOSAL SUBMISSION DECISION

A preliminary review of an RFP should allow you to determine if it is an appropriate grant opportunity for your institution to pursue. You can do this intuitively using the considerations cited above and in chapter 2, or more formally using an RFP decision matrix such as the technique cited below. The RFP decision matrix is also variously known by names such as the comparison matrix, alternatives analysis, bid/no-bid analysis, prioritization matrix, cost/benefit analysis grid, evaluation matrix, multiple dimension comparison matrix, opportunity analysis, option analysis, proposal decision matrix, or Pugh method.

USING A BID/NO-BID RFP DECISION MATRIX

In chapter 3 I introduced a decision tree approach to help an organization decide whether or not grant seeking is an appropriate activity to pursue. A similar approach can be applied to determine whether or not to submit a grant application in response to a specific RFP. A tool to help in this regard, known as the Bid/No-Bid RFP Decision Matrix, has been developed by Technology Evaluation Centers (http://rfptemplates.technologyevaluation.com/Bid-No-Bid -Analysis.html). This organization offers proposal-writing tools and guidance to grant seekers. Their Bid/No-Bid Decision Matrix is shown in figure 6.1.

The bid/no-bid analysis is the assessment of the quantitative and/or qualitative risks inherent in the choice of either submitting or not submitting a grant proposal in response to an RFP. The objective of this analysis is to prevent you from investing your institution's valuable and limited resources in pursuing a grant when your chances of winning are null, very low, or below your institution's established threshold. In applying this matrix, it is useful to empanel two or three staff or board members and have them vote on how your library stacks up against the RFP's award and other weighted criteria.

Furthermore, the fastest and easiest way to increase your ratio of winning proposals is not to send out a proposal in a marginal situation. Indeed, the last thing you want to do is to drain resources from your operations merely for the sake of bidding, so do your homework.

FIGURE 6.1

EXAMPLE OF A BID/NO-BID DECISION MATRIX

		PANEL VOTES	
Criteria	*Weights*	*Bid*	*No Bid*
Project budget realistic	1	2	1
Project time frame realistic	1	3	0
Resources for proposal/bid	1	3	0
Investment needed	1	1	2
Technical expertise	3	3	0
Management expertise	1	2	1
Differentiators from competitors	1	3	0
Information gathering vs. real project	1	1	2
Political considerations	3	0	3
Previous relationship	3	0	3
Project already funded	2	3	0
Scores	18	30	24

Used by permission of Technology Evaluation Centers.

GRANTOR COMMUNICATION AFTER A NO-GO DECISION (KEEPING THE FUTURE DOOR OPEN)

Communication between grantor and grantee is a key factor in any successful procurement system. Therefore, your response to a request for proposal, whether positive or negative, is appreciated by the grantor and will be viewed positively should you want to be considered in future opportunities.

If you decide not to respond to an RFP, it is polite and appropriate to write a one-page letter explaining why your institution decided not to submit a grant application in this instance. The letter should adopt a professional tone and provide one or more good reasons. Express your interest in receiving future RFPs from the granting agency and indicate the point of contact within your organization for future communication.

Technology Evaluation Centers offers this advice in constructing the no-bid letter:

Use a formal letterhead. Do not handwrite your no-bid letter.

First, your no-bid letter should thank the person who sent you the invitation for showing interest in your organization.

Next, state the reasons why you are not proposing a project. Be specific regarding these reasons. This step is the critical factor in remaining on the list of prospective grantors.

Reiterate that you are still interested in being kept informed about new grant opportunities for which your institution may be suited.

Finally, end the letter formally (with "sincerely," for example, or a similar polite expression). Sign your name and indicate your title. Be sure to provide correct and complete contact and reference information for future correspondence. Before sending it, make sure your no-bid letter is tactful, respectful, and goes straight to the point.

Send the no-bid letter to be received before the proposal's delivery deadline date.

Pre-proposal Research
and Fact-Finding

Once you and your advisory panel have analyzed the grant opportunity and decided that the proposal effort is definitely worth a "go," you can initiate your pre-proposal research efforts. Some may ask, "Why bother with research when you have the RFP in hand?" It is my belief (particularly with competitive grants) that you better your chances of winning the grant if your proposal demonstrates a clear understanding of the grantor's goals, your proposed project topic's technical state of the art, and the environmental milieu your proposed project will impact upon. You can obtain this understanding by some good old-fashioned library and Internet research and homework. Analysis of prior awards from a particular grantor may guide you in focusing your project's scope and deciding how much money to ask for.

RESEARCHING THE GRANTOR

Using the information sources cited in chapter 4 and the prospect worksheets in appendix A as guides, gather relevant information on your prospective grantor such as its mission, goals and priorities, prior granting activities, and sources and extent of available grant funding. As cited earlier, good sources for information on foundation grantors are

IRS 990-PF filings   directories/grant indexes

annual reports   grant maker websites

program promotional literature

For government granting agencies at all levels, I find their respective websites are the best sources for current information on their missions and grant programs.

RESEARCHING THE TOPIC

Exercise your reference librarian skills to determine the state of the art of the topical area your project will address, whether it is an advanced computer application, homebound delivery, a youth homework helper program, or community outreach. This will allow you to cite how your project will employ the latest techniques, how your efforts will advance the state of the art, and how your project compares with similar undertakings. This research can also provide you with a lot of good, innovative ideas that you may want to employ in your proposal and project, as well as caveats about problems to avoid. Further, it is good marketing to demonstrate a current awareness of the project topic or problem to be solved in your proposal because this gives reviewers confidence that you will not waste grant money by reinventing the wheel or repeating the mistakes of others. If, based on your research, you believe your project is unique, then state this in your proposal. For example, in a successful 2004 LSTA grant proposal to purchase ten laptop computers to be lent out to senior citizens, my research allowed me to attest that mine would be the first public library in our state and only the second in the United States to lend out laptops.

When scoping out a potential grant, keep in mind that it is generally easier to get a grant to fund a project than to cover general operating expenses.

RESEARCHING THE COMPETITION

When I wrote contract proposals in the highly competitive world of for-profit government contracting, I spent a lot of time trying to identify the competitors who were bidding against us on a specific project and learning how their pricing structures and qualifications compared with those of my company. However, in the not-for-profit grants game, a competitive analysis of this type is not as important or mandatory. Here, institutions are competing for a share of a fixed amount of dollars by submitting proposals for a wide range of projects, with a high probability that no two will be the same. In this not-for-profit milieu, the important competitive datum is the number of institutions you will be competing against vs. the number of grants to be awarded. These data will help you calculate the odds of your proposal being successful. In general, I will not pursue a grant opportunity if I learn in advance that the odds against me are greater than ten to one.

As stated above, you can sometimes get an idea of the number of competitors for a specific grant opportunity at a pre-proposal grant conference by counting heads or from the attendance roster. Also, some government agencies will announce how many letters of intent were received or how many RFPs were requested related to a planned grant award (see below).

ESTIMATING HOW YOUR INSTITUTION STANDS UP AGAINST THE COMPETITION

Although not mandatory in not-for-profit grant seeking, competitive intelligence on those institutions competing against you can be useful. A difficult factor to determine in deciding whether or not to pursue a specific grant, particularly where a highly competitive contest is involved, is how your organization measures up against the competition. However, it may be difficult, if not impossible, to determine whom you are competing with for grant money. Therefore, attend grant pre-conferences when you can. Be observant; study the attendance sheet (usually made public) and read the other attendees' name tags and you will get a good idea of who else may be bidding against you. If there is a limited amount of money to be given away for a specific grant opportunity and there are many grant seekers (some of whom may outclass your institution), you may want to choose your battles and conserve your grant-writing resources for a better opportunity where the playing field may be more level. If you can determine the number of potential applicants, the total amount of grant funds available, and the average grant award value, you can calculate the approximate odds of winning and use this as input in your go/no-go grant bid decision. Many government agencies help in this regard by publicizing the number of LOIs received or the number of RFPs requested. This can help you to calculate the odds of winning a particular grant. To cite an example, a state library announces that it has budgeted $6 million for capital construction grants this year and the maximum grant amount will be $500,000. Therefore, at the maximum award level, at least 12 libraries can receive grants. The state reported that 31 libraries had submitted letters of intent, so the odds of winning are about 1 in 2.6, which are not bad and the grant is worth pursuing. If 120 libraries had expressed interest in bidding, the odds against winning would be 10 to 1 and, in my view, too high to justify a bid based on my personal rule number 3, which is: *Do not pursue a grant opportunity if the odds against your winning are ten to one or more.*

The odds against winning a grant can be significant. For example, in 2009 I participated in a national foundation's library-oriented competitive grant competition. I found out after the fact that I had only 1 in 57 odds of winning, which would have precluded me from bidding had I known this in advance. However, another state library construction grant competition offered three to one odds, which I found to be very attractive.

ATTENDING A PRE-PROPOSAL WORKSHOP

For potentially large (or complex) solicited grants, the grantor may invite potential grant seekers to a pre-proposal workshop either in advance of or at the same time as RFP publication. Some grantors may distribute the RFP only at this conference to ensure that potential grantees attend. Grantors employ the pre-proposal workshop as a means of both ensuring proposal quality and screening potential grantees. In some cases (such as for large government capital construction grant applicants), attendance at a pre-grant workshop or an equivalent webinar may be a mandatory prerequisite to proposal submission. Typical topics discussed at these workshops include criteria for applicant eligibility, desired proposal content and format, submission schedules, and limits on grant expenses and activities.

Whether a requisite or not, it is distinctly to your advantage as a grant seeker to attend a pre-proposal meeting if one is offered. Any information you get there can only make your proposal better. Also, your attendance demonstrates to the grantor that your institution is seriously committed to the prospective grant project. The pre-proposal meeting may also allow you to establish relationships with grantor staff and reviewers. Another benefit of attending a pre-proposal workshop is that it will allow you to size up your competition for the grant by observing your fellow attendees (as they will undoubtedly observe you).

Let me voice a note of caution here, however. Consider all contacts with prospective grant funders to be marketing contacts by which you and your organization may be evaluated. Therefore, behave professionally at pre-bid conferences, do not be a pest, and ask only relevant, genuine, intelligent, and valid questions of the presenters. When chatting with grantor representatives during breaks, be polite and respectful. Do not appear to be giving them a sales pitch or asking for special treatment or privileged information about the RFP or your competition. Remember, a negative pre-proposal impression can harm or even kill your chances of winning a grant.

RFP CLARIFICATION INQUIRIES

When making inquiries to a grantor, the rule is to ask only necessary, intelligent, and relevant questions in accord with my rule number 8: *Don't be a pest to the grantor.* It is okay to ask valid questions regarding issues that are critical to your proposal preparation and submission at a pre-proposal workshop and at any time prior to proposal submission. Valid questions might relate to the rules for joint submissions (i.e., partnering), preferred format, mode of proposal submission, acceptable project costs, requisite project scheduling and reporting, and so on. There is also a caution here too. Before you pose a question to a funding agency, study the RFP to determine whether or not it is answered therein. Grant agency administrators do not think highly of prospective grantees that do not read instructions and bother them unnecessarily. Also, do not ask naive questions which might demonstrate a lack of requisite project-related expertise or experience. Remember, you want the grantor to consider you competent and to look forward to working with you.

Proposal Management and Project Planning

Assigning a good manager and planner ensures a good project. This is true of both your grant application proposal effort and the project it is proposing. Therefore, the first step in a successful grant-seeking strategy is the appointment of a competent proposal manager.

APPOINTING A GRANT PROPOSAL MANAGER

Every grant proposal preparation effort should have an individual who is designated as the proposal manager as stated in my rule number 4: *Appoint a reliable proposal manager.* The proposal manager has the following responsibilities:

- to oversee the entire proposal preparation effort
- to define the proposed project and the proposal
- to build a proposal preparations schedule and budget
- to organize the proposal-writing team
- to assign tasks and obtain necessary resources
- to liaise with the grant maker
- to ensure that the proposal is written in compliance with the RFP and the grantor's instructions, conditions, and requirements

◆ to make sure the proposal package is a complete, high-quality product in both content and format

◆ to ensure that the proposal costs are complete, accurate, and reasonable

◆ to ensure on-time submission and to ensure compliance with all RFP and grantor conditions

As stated in chapter 3, it is advisable that grant-seeking institutions appoint an individual (who could be either paid staff or a volunteer) as a focal point for institutional grant soliciting and marketing activity. This person can also serve as the proposal manager if she offers the requisite management, writing, and technical project skills and has enough time available to devote to proposal preparation tasks. The proposal manager will supervise the tasks outlined below. If the proposed project is relatively small and straightforward (e.g., buying a computer or a range of bookshelves), then proposal writing can be a one-person effort, with a single staff member or volunteer filling all writing roles and serving as her own proposal manager. This approach can work, but, I must caution, always try to have at least one other person review the proposal and final grant application before their submission (see chapter 11). If, on the other hand, you must develop an intricate proposal that defines a multifaceted project, you will need a proposal-writing team of several people. In this case a skilled proposal manager is needed to orchestrate the overall effort. For a major proposal effort, the assigned proposal manager should be extremely reliable in meeting deadlines, have good management and organizational skills, and have enough influence in your organization to requisition the necessary proposal-writing resources and get institutional commitments.

CREATING A PROPOSAL DEVELOPMENT WORK PLAN

The proposal manager and her team will be responsible for designing two project work plans: one for the creation and delivery of the grant application proposal package, and another for the proposed project represented in the proposal. Both will require development of these project elements:

task list	budget
deliverables list	staffing plan
schedule	resources plan

Each of these planning components will be discussed below, for both the proposal and the grant–funded project.

DEVELOPING THE PROPOSAL TASK LIST

The proposal manager will need to define each task in order to achieve the completion and delivery of the grant proposal. The task list will basically include three types of assignments:

- ◆ writing/creating the proposal components
- ◆ reviewing, editing, and proofreading the completed proposal segments
- ◆ production and delivery support

Each task should be given start and end dates, with responsibility for meeting these dates assigned to an individual proposal team member. Figure 8.1 shows an example of how proposal preparation tasks, schedules, and assignments can be integrated into a table, which can then be shared with all team members and used by the proposal manager as a management control tool. Note that in this example the proposal manager has reserved several critical tasks for herself (i.e., writing the executive summary and the management approach; final editing, proofing, and correction; package assembly and production; package delivery; and grantor contact). These are the tasks I typically reserve for myself when I lead a proposal team because I believe it is essential that they be done correctly and I do not feel comfortable in delegating them to others. If you are partnering with one or more organizations that will be providing proposal input, include them in your proposal team, be sure to include their assigned tasks in your work schedule, and make them aware of their assigned deliverables and deadlines.

ESTABLISHING THE PROPOSAL-WRITING AND DELIVERY SCHEDULE

In most cases (and always with solicited proposals) you will be given a deadline for proposal submission, which must be met if your proposal is to be considered (what we called the "drop dead date" in the contracting game). You must comply with the RFP submission schedule and delivery requirements religiously; therefore, my rule number 7 of grant seeking and proposal writing is: *Always meet your submission deadline.* To ensure that the deadline will be met, I usually start with the proposal delivery date and time and work backwards to the present. Develop the scheduled tasks and milestone points from the proposal delivery day and time back to right now, today. List all tasks necessary to complete and deliver the grant proposal and establish a start and completion date for each.

FIGURE 8.1

SAMPLE PROPOSAL WRITING SCHEDULE AND TASK ASSIGNMENT TABLE (THIRTY-DAY CYCLE)

Task/Deliverable	Person Responsible	Task Initiation	First Draft Due	Review Completed	Final Copy	Final Review and Edit	Task Completed
1. Select proposal team and assign tasks	Proposal Manager	Day 1					Day 1
2. Technical approach	Writer 1/Partner	Day 1	Day 14	Day 16	Day 20	Day 21	Day 22
3. Management approach	Proposal Manager	Day 1	Day 16	Day 18	Day 21	Day 21	Day 22
4. Qualifications statement	Writer 2/Partner	Day 1	Day 18	Day 19	Day 20	Day 21	Day 22
5. Appendixes	Writer 3/Partner	Day 5	Day 18	Day 20	Day 21	Day 22	Day 22
6. Cost proposal	Accountant	Day 10	Day 21	Day 22	Day 23	Day 23	Day 24
7. Cover letter	Board President	Day 15	Day 20	Day 21	Day 21	Day 22	Day 22
8. Executive summary	Proposal Manager	Day 19	Day 20	Day 20	Day 21	Day 22	Day 22
9. Graphics support	Staffer 1	As Needed					As Needed
10. Production support	Staffer 2	As Needed					As Needed
11. Final editing, proofing, and correction	Editor/Proposal Manager	As Needed					Day 23
12. Package assembly	Proposal Manager/ Staffer 2	As Needed					Days 25–28
13. Package delivery	Proposal Manager/ Staffer 3	Day 28					Days 28–30
14. Grantor and partner liaison (including post-proposal)	Proposal Manager	As Needed					As Needed

To guide you in this, the task guidelines involved in preparing a typical grant proposal are listed below and are covered in more detail in chapter 10.

Develop a detailed, task-by-task proposal-writing schedule.

Assign proposal tasks to team members and partners with deadlines for drafts and final copy.

Share your overall proposal schedule with all your proposal team members, advising them of the deadlines for drafts, assembly, and submission.

Be aware of competing demands on your team members' time and help them avoid schedule conflicts.

Never give anyone up to the last possible minute to complete a section of the proposal or to provide a necessary attachment.

To allow for contingencies, set the date to have the complete proposal, including all forms, the narrative, the budget, all attachments, and all letters of support, at least four or five days before the day the proposal has to be submitted.

In developing your schedule, note that certain proposal sections may require other sections as inputs, so you may not be able to initiate work on these until you have the information you need from a prior task. An example of this situation is the cost proposal and the executive summary, which will be based on what has been defined in other sections, particularly the technical, management, and qualifications discussions.

DEFINING YOUR PROPOSAL-WRITING BUDGET AND RESOURCE NEEDS

Once you have laid out your proposal's task assignments and production schedule, you will be able to determine what staff and other internal or external resources you will require to complete the proposal (e.g., printing, graphics, computer support, accounting, materiel, hardware, expendables, etc.). This will allow you to then calculate an estimated budget for the proposal's preparation. You will have to think ahead to ensure the proper resources are there when you need them (see below). If you are fortunate enough to be able to find all the proposal-writing and production assets you need within your own institution, then you can write off the costs as overhead and may not have to spend any out-of-pocket cash, even though prudent financial management dictates that you should still be aware of what your proposal will cost so you can apply my rule number 2: *Do not pursue a grant if proposal preparation costs are more than the grant is worth.* A typical government proposal may require about four to five professional person-weeks to prepare. Therefore, it does not make sense to expend this level of effort to request only a $5,000 grant.

LINING UP NEEDED LOGISTICAL SUPPORT IN ADVANCE

Anticipate your proposal's logistical needs so you can arrange for the help you need to be available at the right time. For example, if your proposal is to include special graphics such as illustrations, color work, and tables and graphs, then you may need a graphic artist, graphics software, and a high-quality color printer. If you will need ten copies of a 100-page proposal at the end of the proposal cycle, then give your printing support staff advance warning. If you will be submitting an electronic proposal (see chapter 11), give your information technology department advance notice of the submission date so they can help you package and deliver your e-proposal, and ensure that they will not have to shut down the system for maintenance and repairs just when you're going to need it.

ASSEMBLING THE PROPOSAL-WRITING TEAM AND ASSIGNING WORK

The proposal manager must define every piece of the proposal to be prepared and then assign to team members responsibility for the proposal's writing, compilation, assembly, and delivery. In a typical proposal, the pieces to be written include

cover letter	qualifications statement
cover page	management approach
table of contents	cost proposal
executive summary	appendixes/attachments
technical approach	

Supporting task responsibilities will also need to be assigned. These support tasks include

- technical review, redactory editing, and proofreading
- graphics design and preparation of illustrations, graphs, and tables

- financial and accounting review
- production (hard copy and/or electronic)
- package assembly and delivery
- liaison with grantor and partners

Responsibility for each of these tasks should be assigned to one or more individuals. For a small (e.g., under $10,000) grant, one or two people may be capable of putting together a simple letter or e-mail proposal. However, a major five-, six-, or seven-figure proposal will usually require a team to put the package together. You can select your proposal team members using these six basic grantsmanship criteria:

1. Knowledge of the subject area(s) addressed by the proposal and subsequent project
2. Ability to write flexibly in varying styles
3. Imagination and intellectual organization skill
4. Proven ability to work under pressure
5. Ability to follow instructions
6. Reliability in meeting deadlines

Michael Maccoby in his book *The Gamesman* defines a group of competitive individuals who like to play and win at the corporate game.[1] I have encountered a few of these "gamesmen" and "gameswomen" in my industry experience and have found that they make excellent grantsmen. They enjoy the "thrill of the chase" involved in grant or contract hunting via proposal writing. If you can find this type of individual in your organization and they also write well, then certainly recruit them for your proposal-writing team. They may even thank you for allowing them to exercise their competitive spirit in the service of your library.

Along this same line, Sarah Collins draws upon her twelve years as a grant proposal reviewer (known as a "grant reader" in the trade) to share what she has found to be the common traits of successful proposal writers:[2]

1. Thorough knowledge of the grantor organization and its programs
2. A concise writing style
3. Attention to detail
4. Common sense
5. Empathy with the reader

6. Evident passion for the project to be funded

7. Demonstrated commitment and enthusiasm

If more than one person will be contributing written text or graphics to your proposal, a member of the proposal team should be appointed to serve as an "editor" who will collect these inputs and edit them to ensure consistency of style and adherence to standards. It is advisable for the proposal manager or editor to prepare and distribute to team members a writing style guide to ensure style compatibility and consistency (see chapter 9). You should also line up one or more people to be proofreaders and reviewers at key points and certainly during final editing (see chapter 11).

The proposal manager serves as editor-in-chief, but if she is also a writer of proposal copy, she may be so involved that she may miss errors of commission and omission that an objective, uninvolved person would catch.

Each team member, including the proposal manager, should be provided with a written task assignment. This should define the exact specifications for interim drafts and final "deliverables" and each individual's responsibility toward meeting each deliverable's due date. You should also provide each team member with necessary background information (e.g., the RFP, overall proposal outline, team schedule and task assignments, writing style guide, etc.) and define his or her position in the proposal team's reporting and review structure. The last point is important because sometimes the person designated as proposal manager or editor may have a lower status in your organization's hierarchy than some of the other proposal team members reporting to her. However, for the proposal effort, the proposal manager is in charge. In my government contracting days, this team-versus-corporate leadership-trading concept was known as "flickering authority." Therefore, for the proposal-writing effort, make sure that the proposal manager reports to someone high enough in your library's hierarchy (e.g., the library director) to ensure that the proposal team will get the corporate support it needs.

After convening the proposal team and giving them their assignments, the proposal manager must keep in close touch with each team member to offer assistance and to keep their writing progress on schedule. The proposal manager is the maestro who must ensure that all proposal pieces will harmoniously come together in good tune to meet the delivery deadline. You can only do this by watching and listening to each player and leading from the front like a good concert conductor.

When putting together your proposal team, you may find that your institution lacks certain RFP- or project-required skills or resources or does not satisfy all the eligibility criteria. You can solve this problem and still submit a responsive proposal by partnering on your grant request with another organization that can provide what you need to cover all the bases (see below).

DETERMINING IF YOU NEED A COMPATIBLE PARTNER TO PROVIDE MISSING SKILLS OR ELIGIBILITY

Chapter 4 discussed how certain grants may be restricted to a certain category of organization (e.g., schools, etc.). If you want to pursue these grants but are not eligible, you may need a "strategic partner" to establish a "collective eligibility" to apply for the grant. In other cases, your institution may lack a certain critical skill or resource that is necessary either to bid on the grant or to conduct the proposed project (e.g., statistical survey skills, etc.), so you will need a "technical partner" to provide these skills. In these cases, you will need to apply my rule number 5 of successful grantsmanship: *Find and co-bid with a compatible partner who can provide either the necessary eligibility or expertise.* Even when it is not a necessity, partnering can be a good grant-marketing strategy. Grant makers like to see the primary grant requester increase the probability of project success by including a qualified partner or two to strengthen the proposed project team. It also allows the grantor to feel it is "spreading the wealth around" by aiding two or more needy and worthy institutions instead of just one.

You can generally select between three basic types of partners: (1) a co-beneficiary, such as another public library, who will share the grant effort, grant funding, and grant benefits with you; (2) a strategic partner who provides needed project skills or resources that are not available at your library; or (3) a strategic partner who will provide "collective eligibility" to receive the grant. Partners come in all flavors. They can be institutions or individuals, not-for-profits or businesses, local or distant. Their participation should be in accord with a clearly defined role (in writing) and should yield clearly defined benefits (in addition to meeting eligibility criteria), such as improved results, cost savings, or avoidance of duplication of effort. You may have to pay your strategic partner for their contribution to the project, but if they will provide their efforts on a full or partial pro bono basis, this should be clearly stated, as it really strengthens your proposal. You may also be able to include the dollarized value of their pro bono contribution in your cost proposal as a "shared cost " or "matching cost."

If you intend to partner on a grant project, then you will need to assure the grantor that you and your partner(s) will be able to work together efficiently. Therefore cite any agreement between you and your partner relevant to the project. It is wise to approach any partnering relationship in a businesslike contractual manner. Avoid oral handshake agreements, and document your partnering plans with a formal written agreement that you can include in your proposal. A strong partnership agreement should cover

- project details, including scope and period of performance
- specific partner project roles and responsibilities, and the services to be provided
- levels of effort (person-hours) to be provided
- in-kind resources to be provided
- principal points of contact
- reporting and liaison
- names of individuals to be employed and chain of command
- project deliverable responsibility, deadlines, and ownership
- compensation for labor and expenses
- publicity and public recognition
- mode of continuing cooperation beyond the grant project (sustainability)

I can cite one of my library's LSTA grants as an example of a successful partnership. The grant was for improving library services to seniors and the homebound. The state library's RFP required that the project include a survey and a statistical outcome-based evaluation task to validate that stated goals were achieved. My library staff did not possess the skills necessary to perform this task, but we were able to enlist the help of a research institute at a Penn State University branch campus near us. The institute's director himself contributed to the proposal, designed the proposed survey instruments, and offered to analyze the survey results, all on a pro bono basis. The state granting agency was delighted at this university/public library partnership and we won the grant. On another grant proposal to set up a public library "outpost" in a nearby town, my library partnered with a redevelopment association that agreed to donate a piece of its downtown real estate to house the outpost.

If the proposed activity involves contributions from more than one agency, each partner must also be included in the proposal development process. If you are expecting proposal input from partner agencies, volunteers, or board members, take their schedules into account. Request any information you will need from partners (data, text, graphics, qualifications, biographies, support letters, budgetary needs, etc.) early in the proposal preparation cycle so you won't have to press them for a crucial document when you're down to the wire.

If you do intend to partner on your grant, get formal letters of commitment from your partner(s) and include them in the grant application package that you submit. Document your understanding with your partners in a separate contractual letter which should include their specific roles both in the proposal effort and the subsequent project, the specific deliverables each partner must provide and schedules for these submissions, whom they will report to, and their compensation if any. Documenting everything in writing via mutual letters of agreement will avoid any misunderstandings and give you a "contract" document to share with grantors as needed.

UNDERSTANDING THE PROPOSAL REVIEW PROCESS

It is good marketing and common sense to design your proposal submission package in response to the RFP and its criteria. If you also design your product for its intended target audience readers, you ensure that it will be well received and the grant reviewer's decision making will be made easier. Understanding the proposal review process will help you to write better proposals.

The winning of grants is a form of contest between the proposal submitter and the proposal reviewer. In any contest, your chance of winning is improved if you know and understand the other side's strategy. Therefore, your chance of winning at the grants game is greatly improved if you understand how a grant maker's reviewers evaluate and rank the proposals they receive. By structuring your proposal to readily mesh with the reviewer's technique, you make his job easier and in most cases you score higher. Culick, Godard, and Terk provide valuable insight into how reviewers think when they define the six basic steps in due diligence to be undertaken by a proposal reviewer:[3]

1. Review grant proposal, budget, and supplemental documents

   ◆ Review proposal for fit with foundation's mission, guidelines, and strategy
   ◆ Familiarize yourself with the basics of the proposed project and the organization
   ◆ Review supplemental materials, such as strategic plans, financial reports, marketing materials, staff biographies, and so on
   ◆ Assess strength of the project's focus and design
   ◆ Consider the viability of the project budget and overall financial health

2. Conduct additional preliminary research
   - Ask colleagues (funders and other experts in the field) for their input
   - Review the organization's website
   - Seek out other available data and information relevant to the project

3. Conduct interviews with organization's leadership (site visit or phone)
   - Get to know the executive director, key program staff, and board leadership
   - Explore the organization's health and capacity, including track record, governance and executive leadership, vision and strategy, staffing, partnerships, communications, and finance
   - Delve more deeply into the proposed project, focusing on planning, outcomes, and evaluation

4. Conduct additional follow-up research as needed
   - Probe areas of concern through additional research and discussions with colleagues and staff or board leadership

5. Analyze and apply your due diligence findings
   - Consider "red flags" and assess the risk they pose to the success of the project
   - Weigh the factors important to your organization; determine if there are any "deal breakers"
   - Consider options for structuring the grant
   - Make decision about grant

6. Synthesize information and present to others
   - Write up due diligence findings and decision
   - Craft finding recommendation for staff and board review

I present these due diligence pointers because I believe that we grantsmen and grantswomen will tend to fare better in our grant seeking if we can empathize with the grant makers and especially with those individuals who review proposals and make the award decisions.

RESPONSIVENESS TO THE RFP

One of the most important jobs of the proposal manager is designing the proposal package and defining its scope. Following rule number 6 of proposal writing, *Read the grantor's instructions and give them exactly what they want*, begin this task by carefully reading the grantor's solicitation (RFP). Before starting any work, make sure you know what the RFP specifies as (a) mandatory submissions and (b) allowable optional submissions. You don't want your proposal to be tossed out as ineligible because you left out a mandatory submission element, nor do you want to lose points (or be declared ineligible) because your proposal included something that was forbidden or that violated certain submission specifications regarding format, size, or scope. Everything required in the application should be in the body of the proposal, not in an attachment, unless the RFP disallows this. Send everything at the same time—don't send supplemental information later.

CREATING A GOOD TABLE OF CONTENTS

A good way to start defining your proposal's format, structure, and content is to create a proposal table of contents to serve as a road map for subsequent proposal writing. Some RFPs can be very specific as to the proposal's format and structure, specifying section headings, points to be addressed, and page, word, or character count limits per section. If specific proposal data elements are required by the RFP (e.g., project results and deliverables, target populations definition, project staffing, schedules and budgets, etc.), then build these into your contents outline and ensure that each has a labeled section in the submitted application document. This will allow reviewers to quickly determine that you have been responsive to the RFP as they go through their checklist, and this can win you points. Don't omit anything that is called for in the solicitation. Even if a requested information element is not relevant to your organization, respond in the appropriate section by stating "not applicable" or something similar. An important, even if unstated, criterion for most granting institutions in selecting their grantees is demonstrated responsiveness and the ability of the potential grantee to follow instructions. Therefore, check to see what the RFP allows and requires and *give 'em the contents they want.*

You might want to consider a technique I have employed. This is to extract from the RFP, *verbatim*, all mandatory section headings, specifications, and rules. I then incorporate these phrases and rules into my proposal's table of contents and also into the proposal style guide. If you have a digital RFP, you can do this via highlighting, copying, and pasting the terms into your proposal draft. I believe that using the grantor's own words from the RFP in your proposal is not only good marketing but helps the proposal reviewers in evaluating your submission and may help improve your score.

For example, if the RFP specifies that you include in your proposal a section containing "Proposed Project Staff Resumes," do not be cute and label it instead "Project Team Biographies." Rewording may demonstrate your thesaurus skills, but it may also lose you points with reviewers. It is likely that the folks who evaluate your grant proposal are the same ones who wrote the grant solicitation document. They may not appreciate your rewriting their words, but conversely will take your acceptance of their language as a positive sign of cooperativeness. Simply stated, in proposal writing the more closely you follow their rules and demonstrate your acceptance and understanding of the grantor's priorities and purposes, the higher your probability of success.

As stated above, you can ensure that your proposal's format and structure follow the RFP's specifications by first creating an overall proposal outline that incorporates all of the RFP's required sections as proposal chapter headings. Do not be afraid to use the RFP's words and language, as this will demonstrate to reviewers that you have read the RFP and are being responsive to it. By providing proposal section headings corresponding to each mandatory RFP datum, you make it easy for the reviewer (and you) to tick these off and confirm that your proposal is indeed responsive to the RFP in every aspect. By inadvertently leaving out a required section in a proposal you will, at best lose points and, at worst, cause your proposal to be rejected as being nonresponsive.

In this vein, I have also found it useful to analyze the RFP's text to see which "buzzwords" or phrases are employed with the most frequency in the grantor's stated mission, goals, and objectives. For example, a recent RFP was issued by a corporate foundation to solicit proposals for community support activities. I found that this RFP's text used each of the following terms ten or more times: "community development," "special group needs," "outreach," and "cultural diversity." I incorporated each of these terms into my proposal. Make a list of grantor buzzwords and phrases and, if you can without appearing awkward, incorporate them into your proposal, particularly in the executive summary and statement of needs sections.

When developing your table of contents, also consider your placement of graphics, appendixes, and attachments in the proposal. Determine if graphics may be included (e.g., can or must you include tables, graphs, photos, etc.) and if graphics should either be integrated into the narrative text or included as attachments at the end. Include only permitted attachments which you deem necessary to respond to an RFP requirement, prove a technical point, or demonstrate your institution's eligibility or qualifications. Typical proposal attachments are statistical tables, news clippings, annual reports, financial reports, biographies, tax-exempt determination, strategic plan excerpts, and so on.

Some RFPs give the applicant a choice of submission physical formats (e.g., hard copy, fax, electronic, etc.), while others specify only one format. Be sure to give them what they want. Electronic submission format is becoming the most common type (75 percent of the grant proposals I prepared in 2009 were electronic). These online submissions can be a little tricky until mastered, especially if mandatory word or character count limits are specified and tables or graphics are to be inserted. Therefore, you may want to ensure that someone skilled in computer word processing is available when you prepare and submit your digital proposal, in order to provide troubleshooting advice. For example, on my first electronic proposal submission to our state library in 2004, I was assisted by our county's public library district consultant, who guided me in putting together and submitting the digital document.

Guidelines on packaging and delivering your proposal, whether digital or hard copy, will be found in chapter 11.

Occasionally, you may be called upon to write a grant proposal for which there is no prespecified format. If so, do not despair. You can apply and adapt what I term the "standard discretionary proposal format." Using this or whichever other format outline you employ, you will have to make sure that your proposal clearly states the *Why, What, How,* and *Who* of your proposed project. The standard proposal format below does this. I have evolved and successfully employed it both as a public library "grantsman" and in my prior life as a "Beltway bandit" government contract proposal writer. Note that when a brief letter proposal is appropriate, you will want to hit most of these same points as well but in an abbreviated way.

Each of the following "standard" proposal outline elements is elaborated upon in chapter 10:

1. Cover/transmittal letter (specifying contact person and signed by an officer)
2. Title page
3. Overview and executive summary (write this last)
4. Statement of need (the problem to be solved by the grant; *Why?* and *Who?*; statement of project goals and objectives)
5. Technical approach (project details and methods; solution to the problem; *What?*)
6. Results evaluation criteria and methods (proof the grant money was well spent)
7. Management proposal (schedule, staffing, resources; *How?*)
8. Cost proposal (how much you want plus any cost sharing)

9. Qualifications statement (why they should award the grant to you)

10. Promotion plans (good publicity for grantor and grantee)

11. Appendixes (supporting data such as resumes, clippings, financial reports, etc.)

PRE-SUBMISSION CONTACT WITH GRANTOR

If unsure how to respond to a particular RFP requirement, contact the granting agency to ask for clarification. I have found that asking valid questions during the proposal-writing phase may actually help in building rapport. However, let me provide a word of caution here. (Remember rule number 8: *Do not be a pest.*) Ask only relevant, genuine, intelligent, and valid questions. It is okay to ask questions about proposal submission procedures or formats, but do not ask for advice on a "technical" matter on which you should be knowledgeable, such as on the operation of a public library. Posing a naive query can hurt you by creating doubt in an evaluator's mind about your understanding and ability to successfully conduct the project. Also keep in mind that some of the smaller foundations may employ ad hoc reviewers, and they do not have staff available to talk with you about your proposal.

REQUESTING SAMPLE PROPOSALS

Some granting agencies may provide, on request, sample copies of prior winning proposals submitted to them. This is usually true of government agencies where the successful proposal often becomes part of the grantor's public domain contract file upon grant award. For example, the Institute of Museum and Library Services' website actually has a link to successful "sample applications": www.imls.gov/applicants/sample.shtm.

NOTES

1. Michael Maccoby, *The Gamesman: The New Corporate Leaders* (New York: Bantam Books, 1978).

2. Sarah Collins, ed., *The Foundation Center's Guide to Winning Proposals* (New York: Foundation Center, 2006), vii.

3. Liza Culick, Kristen Godard, and Natasha Terk, *The Due Diligence Tool for Use in Pre-Grant Assessment* (Washington, DC: Grantmakers for Effective Organizations, 2004), 8.

Proposal Writing Style

A grant proposal is a fairly stylized piece of marketing literature which may be characterized as a cross between a technical report and a sales brochure. The grant-seeking institution is selling its credentials and its project's value to a grantor who has funds to support good works. If the grant process is competitive, the grant proposal must also convince the reviewers that the grant-requesting institution and its proposed project are more worthy of the grant than those of other competing institutions. Your grant proposal is often all the review panel will employ to make their award decisions, so it must tell your whole story in a clear, concise, and convincing manner.

STYLE TIPS

You should recognize that your grant proposal is a marketing document. You are competitively selling your institution, its needs, and its qualifications to one or more grant reviewers. Since the best salespeople are those who empathize with their customers, write your proposal with the needs of the reviewers in mind. You can facilitate the review of your proposal by giving it a straightforward logical format, labeling all sections, writing in a clear, concise, simple style, and avoiding jargon. You want your proposal to convince the reviewer that awarding your institution a grant will yield a highly successful project that will reflect positively on both the grantor and grantee. The style pointers below will help you to write a proposal to accomplish this result.

Keeping It Simple

The first and foremost thing to keep in mind is the KIS principle, "Keep It Simple." Use short paragraphs and strong topical sentences. Use bullet points to list important facts. Explain anything that is not obvious. Do not assume that reviewers are familiar with your organization, service area, or the needs of your community. Sarah Collins, an experienced grant reviewer, warns against proposal complexity when she states that "an idiosyncratic proposal format signaled [to the reviewer] larger problems with a nonprofit applicant."[1] Collins also cautions against being too rigid in responding to an RFP and advises flexibility in choosing the best way to sell your program to the funder.

The sheer volume of proposals that most foundations receive means that your proposal will initially be read quickly. Simple sentence structures, short paragraphs beginning with strong topical sentences, and important facts broken out in bullet points will best reveal the proposal's main points and help advance it to a more in-depth reading by the reviewer.

I am not suggesting that you dumb down the proposal or define every technical term. What I do recommend is that you write your proposals on a level that shows respect for your audience and your ability to communicate your case to a lay audience. The experts will be impressed, not put off, by your ability to explain complex issues in simple terms. The lawyer portrayed by Denzel Washington in the movie *Philadelphia* was fond of saying: "Explain it to me like I'm a six-year-old." You don't have to go that far, but it's a good phrase to remember. When I started my career as a young research librarian at AT&T's Bell Labs, I was instructed to follow Robert Gunning's principles of clear writing in my business and technical writing.[2] "Gunning's fog index" is a test designed to measure a document's readability. The fog index number indicates the number of years of formal education that a person requires in order to easily understand the text on the first reading. If a passage has a fog index of 12, it has the reading level of a twelfth-grade U.S. high school senior. The fog index is generally used by people who want their writing to be read easily by a large segment of the population. Texts that are designed for a wide audience generally require a fog index of less than 12. Texts that require a close-to-universal understanding generally require an index of 8 or less. Since I do not know who will actually be reading the proposals I write, I strive to keep the fog index at level 8.

Developing Descriptive and Catchy
Project and Goal Titles

It is both good writing and good marketing technique to come up with a descriptive and catchy title for your grant project that will appeal to reviewers and make them want to read your proposal. An interesting title will also be handy to use in press releases and reports after you win the grant. It is also good style to apply this rule to the titles of your stated project goals and individual tasks. For example, instead of naming your project "Computer Courses for Senior Citizens," why not term it "Computer Skills for Technologically Handicapped Older Adults"?

Using Simple, Declarative, Positive Sentences

When you write, concentrate on producing simple, clear, declarative sentences. Do not obfuscate. Leave out emotion and hype. Be precise. I have found that a proposal's narrative comes across better if written as short precise statements in a positive, forceful, and declarative mode. Use action verbs such as *will* and *shall* in first-person plural, future tense. Examples are statements such as "In month one we (or the XYZ Library) will perform the following tasks . . . ," "Phase one shall be the implementation of . . . ," or "In this task we will define (or investigate, or create, or evaluate, etc.) . . ." Remember, faint heart never won fair grant. Write with confidence, as if you are certain the proposed project will be successful. Avoid "iffy" qualifying phrases such as "we hope," "hopefully," "with luck," "maybe," or "if possible." A proposal that exudes uncertainty or a lack of confidence will not likely be a winner.

Avoiding Your Own Jargon

You should always make an effort to avoid jargon. That includes not only your library's in-house jargon but also the jargon common to your field. You cannot be certain that your proposal's reviewers are experts in your field, and you want them to understand what you are proposing to do. For example, I have stopped using the phase "my library's collections" because I found that non-librarians thought I was discussing fund-raising (I now say "my library's collection of books").

Some advisors on grant writing suggest that you should eschew even the jargon used by the funder in the RFP and translate RFP jargon into plain language. I disagree on this point. I believe that by employing the funder's language in your proposal, you demonstrate both that you have read the guidelines and that you will be a responsive and adaptive grantee. My marketing sense tells me that if you want to use the grantor's money, then you must play by the grantor's rules and use his language.

Being Consistent and Complete

Make sure the information and wording in each table, chart, and attachment is consistent with the proposal narrative and the information in other tables. Your budget line items should reflect back to the proposed activities. All required forms should be filled in accurately and completely. Use consistent language when describing things or processes. For example, while textual variety is nice for creative or literary writing, calling the people who visit your library by differing names in different parts of your proposal (e.g., patrons, customers, users, readers, clientele, etc.) may serve only to confuse reviewers.

Writing for Your Audience

When writing, just as when speaking, address your audience. "Audience" does not just mean the program officer who will first read your proposal or the peer reviewer panel that will rank it. It means everyone who will read it, possibly including foundation management and trustees. Therefore, write for a wider audience than just program officers and technical reviewers alone. Chances are that the executives who are ultimate decision makers are going to read at least some of your proposal.

Striving for a Conversational Tone

A conversational tone automatically eliminates long, winding sentences and excessive jargon. You do not speak that way, so there is no reason to write that way. I suggest that proposal writers imagine they are explaining the what, why, and how of the proposed project to a friend or relative (e.g., a favorite uncle or aunt). A conversational tone helps establish the sense of personal contact with the reader. Individuals, not faceless institutions, make grants, and connecting person-to-person is critical in making a persuasive case for funding. Read the entire proposal aloud, sentence by sentence. If it does not sound right or you cannot finish a sentence on one breath, more work is needed to simplify and shorten. If possible, read your proposal aloud to a friend outside the profession, gauge her reactions, and revise your proposal accordingly. Alternately, have someone from outside your organization read your proposal to make sure it holds the reader's interest and that your message is clear.

Being Brief

In *Hamlet* Shakespeare has Polonius profess, "Brevity is the soul of wit." I think that grant proposal reviewers appreciate this advice. They have many words to review, and more is not better in this context.

Using Proper Physical Format

Unless otherwise specified, use large type (12-point), double-spaced; use one side of 20-pound white paper; provide reasonable margins; number the pages and employ an easy-to-use removable binding (e.g., binder clips). Section divider tabs are not commonly used.

Using Graphics to Strengthen Your Case

If graphics are allowed in the proposal, you can effectively use statistical tables, charts, graphs, photos, news clippings, and organization charts to illustrate and support your case. These are useful and can reduce verbiage in the text, but they must be relevant, labeled, and cited in the appropriate section of the text. Color is nice (if it really adds something), but use caution when including graphics in an e-proposal. Too much graphics and color can complicate transmission, storage, display, and printing for both you and the reviewers

Miscellaneous Style Pointers

Here are some miscellaneous style pointers that I have found to be useful guidelines in writing proposals:

- Maintain reader interest by starting with a question and then answering it.
- Use language familiar to the funder; repeat back the language of the RFP.
- Be logical and linear in approach.
- Observe page and section limitations (especially in e-proposals).

- ◆ Reviewers can consider only the information in the application, so make no assumptions about what they do and don't know.
- ◆ If you're unable to provide any required information, be honest about the reasons for the omission.

NOTES

1. Sarah Collins, ed., *The Foundation Center's Guide to Winning Proposals* (New York: Foundation Center, 2006), xi.

2. Robert Gunning, *The Technique of Clear Writing* (New York: McGraw-Hill, 1952).

Proposal Writing Section by Section

Although each grant RFP and proposal may have its own unique features, they also have much in common. Virtually all proposals will contain a mix of the segments I have listed in the standard discretionary proposal format outlined below. Therefore, in this chapter we will look at the factors to be considered in preparing each of these sections:

1. Cover/transmittal letter (specifying contact person and signed by an officer)

2. Title page

3. Table of contents

4. Overview and executive summary (write this last)

5. Statement of need (the problem to be solved by the grant; *Why?* and for *Whom?*; project goals and objectives)

6. Technical approach (project details and methods; solution to the problem; *What?*; response to the need)

7. Results evaluation criteria and methods (proving that the grant money was well spent; how we will know we have accomplished what we set out to do)

8. Management proposal (schedule, staffing, resources; *When?* and by *Whom?*)

9. Cost proposal (how much you want plus any cost sharing)

10. Qualifications statement (why they should award the grant to you)

11. Promotion plan (good publicity for grantor and grantee)

12. Appendixes (supporting data such as resumes, news clippings, financial reports, etc.)

COVER/TRANSMITTAL LETTER

A one-page cover/transmittal letter on nice letterhead should accompany every proposal submission. If you have letterhead that lists your trustees, use that because some of them may be known to the grant-funding agency, and relationships are always helpful in grant seeking. If delivered by other than the U.S. Postal Service, then indicate at the top of the letter (under your institution's name and address and above the date) the mode of proposal submittal (e.g., "by hand," "via fax," etc.). The cover letter should be addressed to the granting agency's contact person specified in the RFP and should reference the RFP's title, number, and date. If your proposal is unsolicited, clearly state that this is a request for grant funding. Cite prior contacts with the grantor. The name of the project should also be stated (using a catchy descriptive phrase if possible), preferably in a subject block at the top of the page before the salutation. If not obvious, briefly describe the nature of your organization and its background. Summarize the purpose of the requested funding and the amount of your request in the first paragraph. The letter should be dated with the actual proposal submittal date, if different than the proposal due date. Be sure to include your organization's contact person's name and address along with his telephone, fax numbers, and e-mail address. Conclude with an offer to meet, answer questions, and provide more information. Figure 10.1 illustrates a typical proposal cover letter.

TITLE PAGE

Each proposal (with the exception of letter proposals) should have a well-laid-out (not cramped) title cover page presenting these information elements:

1. Project title (descriptive and catchy)

2. Name, address, phone, fax numbers, and e-mail of proposal submitter

FIGURE 10.1

EXAMPLE OF A TYPICAL PROPOSAL COVER LETTER

Milanof-Schock Library

A Free Public Library Serving East Donegal Township, Marietta Borough,
Mount Joy Borough, Mount Joy Township, and Rapho Township

1184 Anderson Ferry Road
Mount Joy, PA 17552-9723

Herbert B. Landau
Library Director
Phone (717) 653-1510
Fax (717) 653- 6590
landau@mountjoy.lib.pa.us

Old Mill Foundation
Administrative Assistant
99 E. King Street, Room 14
Lancaster, Pa 17602

(VIA HAND DELIVERY)

24 March 20XX

SUBJECT: 20XX Grant Request

REFERENCE: *Lancaster New Era* Article of November 15, 20XX
Requesting Grant Applications

Gentlepeople:

The Milanof-Schock Library is pleased to submit the enclosed application for a
20XX Ressler Mill Foundation grant for funds to conduct a bicycle safety event for
our community's children and teenagers. As requested, we have also included:

1. A copy of our IRS 501(c)(3) determination letter;
2. An official Board resolution in support of the request;
3. Copies of our 20XX audited financial statement and 20XX
   year-end financial report;
4. A roster of our Board of Directors and Officers; and
5. Selected literature relevant to the request.

Please do not hesitate to contact me should you have any questions or if you
would like to meet with us to discuss the request.
Thank you for your consideration.

Sincerely,

Herbert B. Landau
Library Director
Encl:

3. Submitter logo (optional)

4. Submitter contact person

5. Grantor corporate name, personal delivery contact name, phone number, and point of delivery address

6. RFP title, number, and date

7. Proposal submittal date

Figure 10.2 illustrates a typical proposal cover page.

FIGURE 10.2

EXAMPLE OF A TYPICAL PROPOSAL COVER PAGE

APPLICATION FOR LSTA GRANT
TO IMPROVE LIBRARY SERVICES TO
TECHNOLOGICALLY HANDICAPPED AND
HOMEBOUND SENIOR PATRONS

SUBMITTED TO:
CONRAD CARD CATALOG
LSTA ADMINISTRATOR
PENNSYLVANIA DEPARTMENT OF EDUCATION
OFFICE OF COMMONWEALTH LIBRARIES
33 MARKET STREET
HARRISBURG, PA 17126-1745

September 5, 2009

By The
Milanof-Schock Library
1184 Anderson Ferry Road
Mount Joy, PA 17552
717 653 1510
717 653 6590 (Fax)
landau@mountjoy.lib.pa.us

Herbert B. Landau
Library Director

FIGURE 10.3

EXAMPLE OF A TYPICAL PROPOSAL TABLE OF CONTENTS

TABLE OF CONTENTS

If your proposal has a number of chapters, include a table of contents to assist the reader in navigating the document. List all sections and chapters and their beginning pages in the table of contents. Figure 10.3 illustrates a typical proposal table of contents.

OVERVIEW AND EXECUTIVE SUMMARY

The proposal's overview and executive summary is a concise abstract or thumbnail of the entire proposed project. It should tell the whole story in microcosm. It is not an introduction. Write it last, after all other sections have been completed, to ensure it is accurate and comprehensive. Some may say that this is the most important section of your proposal and deserves the most attention. When I was a government contractor and writing proposals for a living, my boss advised me to take particular care in writing the executive summary and the management and cost sections. His twenty years of experience had convinced him that 90 percent of funding decisions would be made by the time the reviewer finishes reading these sections. He believed that proposal evaluators and many high-level administrators in a hurry look only at these parts. Indeed, there is a belief among many proposal writers that some reviewers use the overview and executive summary to decide whether the rest of the proposal is worth reading. Therefore, make sure you follow the three "Cs" of being *concise, compelling,* and *clear* in writing this proposal chapter.

If the RFP does not specify size, limit your executive summary to one to two pages (about 250–500 words).

The overview and executive summary's structure should mirror the structure of your proposal by addressing these points in summary format:

+ Communities and population served by your institution
+ Statement of need and proposed solution (the proposed project's scope and purpose)

What you will accomplish

Why it's important

Who will benefit

+ Project importance (highlighting impacted communities)
+ Project relevance to funder's mission
+ Proposed project organization and partners
+ Resource and staffing requirements
+ Proposed project budget summary
+ Proposed project schedule
+ Results, outcomes, and deliverables expected
+ Your institutional history, mission, and background
+ Your qualifications and recognition relevant to the proposed project

---

STATEMENT OF NEED, OR
THE PROBLEM TO BE SOLVED

The proposal's statement of need should clearly state the "why" and "who" of the proposed grant as it relates to communities and people. Here you develop an effective, well-documented argument as to why the project is necessary. State the problem or problems within your community that the proposed grant project will address and solve and who will benefit. It is effective to go from general to specific in developing your case (what some call the funnel approach). Start with the generalized problem as it occurs in your community and work your way down to the specifics. Outline your current resources that address this problem and identify gaps in those resources. State how your proposed project will fill these gaps. Use hard facts and figures where you can to support your statement of need. For example, if you are requesting a grant to fund the establishment of an after-school teen program in your library, you can start your problem definition by presenting statistics on the number of teens in your community and the lack of teen centers and after-school programs for them, along with numbers demonstrating an increase in juvenile delinquency arrests and court cases. Then you can explain how your proposed program will get the teens off the streets and into wholesome educational activities, thereby reducing the likelihood of their getting into trouble. You can give a cursory description of the planned teen activities, but save the details for the technical approach section discussed below.

State and describe your project's goals and objectives using what the Foundation Center terms the "SMART" technique: Specific, Measurable, Achievable, Realistic, Timebound.

To the extent possible, relate the needs addressed by the proposed project and its expected outcome to the granting agency's mission and purpose. A thorough knowledge of the grantor's goals can be a great asset here. It also helps to cite projected "community impact" statistics, such as the number of library patrons and specific members of the community who will benefit from the proposed project. Highlight any beneficiary groups that may also be within the focus of the granting agency, such as seniors, minorities, immigrants, handicapped, preschoolers, and so on. Since "outcome-based results" is now a popular concept among granting agencies, stating needs in terms of expected results can be effective in this section as well as in the evaluation section discussed below.

If you can, jazz up your statements here with some sales-oriented verbiage. For example, if you are requesting grant monies to purchase instructional computers, you can start by discussing "the need for improved adult education in our community for special populations who are *technologically handicapped*" rather than just stating "we require 20 Model XYZ30 desktops for our computer lab."

TECHNICAL APPROACH

The technical approach section presents the *What* and *How* of the proposed grant project. In the preceding statement of need section you defined a problem that needs to be solved. The technical approach section tells in detail how you intend to solve that problem. Here is where you define each of the project's specific tasks, their sequence, interrelationships, and expected results. This section presents methods and schedules and defines what actions you will take to achieve your proposed project's goals and achieve success. Grantors like projects that can serve as "models," perfecting techniques that can be employed by others. Therefore, express here how institutions with similar needs and communities can replicate your project's success.

Even though your project may be complex, empathize with the reader here and try to keep the description simple, straightforward, and clear (remember Gunning's fog index). As stated in chapter 9 on writing style, avoid arcane jargon but do provide a sufficient level of technical detail. If the proposal is to your state library, such as a request for an LSTA grant, the evaluators will most likely be librarians, so a modicum of library science-related detail and terminology is acceptable. However, if your grant request is to a community philanthropic foundation, then library jargon should be eschewed and explanations of basic public library operations should be given. Even the simplest jargon may be confusing. For example, when we librarians speak of weeding, many lay people think we are talking about our landscaping.

Remember that your proposal is a marketing document, and as you develop your technical project approach, it is useful to relate its tasks to the goals of the project as you have defined them in your statement of need. For example, let us say that the goal of your grant is to improve library service to seniors and therefore includes initiating the delivery of library materials to the homebound. Rather than simply stating "In Task 4 we will acquire a vehicle to facilitate homebound delivery," you can, alternatively, schmaltz this up a bit and state: "In Task 4 we will acquire our 'Reads on Wheels' van, which will be specially outfitted to deliver large-type books, audiobooks, periodicals, and audiovisuals to homebound seniors and shut-ins both at home and in assisted-living facilities." Do not be subtle about important points such as the community's need for the project and its anticipated benefits. If appropriate, cite any potential harm to the community by not performing the project. For example, "without this youth involvement project, teen delinquency in River City may increase."

The technical approach section is the core of your proposal and describes exactly what you plan to do on your proposed project. To develop a complete technical approach description, you must first conceptualize your project step-by-step. I have found a helpful way to do this is by developing a "logical project task sequence outline." From this you can write in task details and then derive the project's resource requirements, budget, and schedule, which will be presented in other proposal chapters. If the RFP specifies an overall proposal outline, incorporate this into your logical sequential task outline as a road map for your proposed project's technical implementation steps. Developing this type of outline is discussed below.

DEVELOPING A LOGICAL PROJECT TASK
SEQUENCE OUTLINE

Here is a logical construct you can employ to develop your task definition model. Most grant proposals are requests to fund a specific project. The project will involve a series of interrelated tasks to be performed over a specific period of time. To accomplish these tasks, you will require skilled people who will need resources such as materiel and facilities. In order for you to develop a comprehensive and logical proposal, it is important that you think out the proposed project step-by-step and task-by-task. You must then link the tasks via a logical outline or flow chart. Then, for each task, determine the requisite resources needed in terms of labor, materiel, and space. For each task, define necessary information inputs and output "deliverables" such as reports, programs, workshops, reference inquiries, books purchased, and so on. Then calculate the elapsed timetable (or period of performance) necessary to complete each task. Task sequencing is an important consideration because certain tasks may be prerequisites to others, and it may be necessary to conduct some tasks in parallel to meet RFP or project-mandated deadlines. Finally, a cost figure will then be calculated for each sequential task and these task costs can be compiled into a project budget. Project scheduling and costing will be discussed in further detail below.

The resulting task summary is a road map which can then serve as the outline for the proposed project, its technical proposal, and sequential schedule. These data can be used to produce a handy one-page summary of the entire proposal and project to guide both the proposal-writing team and the grant reviewers.

When I wrote proposals for a living, building a one-page logical task summary like this was the first thing I did when I decided to respond to an RFP. It kept my proposal-writing team and me on target and demonstrated to reviewers that my proposed project was well thought out. A practice I like to follow in naming specific proposed project tasks in the logical project task sequence outline is to use action verbs (e.g., develop, build, create, design, implement, conduct, teach, etc.) which, I believe, presents a positive and goal-oriented impression to writers and reviewers.

A very useful adjunct to this task outline is a milestone schedule, also known as a Gantt chart, which lays out the major project tasks in parallel time tracks, showing all major milestones (what we called "deliverables" in the government contracting game). You can draw your Gantt charts manually or use one of the many tools to create a Gantt chart via computer. For example, there is the Microsoft Project Task-Planning Program, which makes it easy to track and chart project time lines with a built-in Gantt chart view. Another option is to use

MS Excel software. Although Excel does not contain a built-in Gantt chart format, you can create a Gantt chart in Excel by customizing the stacked-bar chart type. There are also a variety of Gantt chart software packages available on the Internet such as Viewpath, SmartDraw, and so on.

Figures 10.4 and 10.5 show examples of a logical project task sequence outline (with budget figures) and a Gantt milestone chart from a successful $45,560 LSTA grant proposal my library submitted to the Pennsylvania Commonwealth Libraries in 2004. This grant funded a project to provide computer instruction and homebound delivery service to senior citizens in our library's service area. On the milestone chart in figure 10.5, note that one can show elapsed time by either using actual month names or "Month 1," Month 2," and so on instead of actual dates if an exact starting date is not known at proposal-writing time.

RESULTS EVALUATION CRITERIA

To inspire confidence among evaluators, your proposal should include a section on how you will evaluate project results against project objectives. This will assure the granting agency that the positive impact of their grant will be objectively measured and reported. Indeed, more and more grantors now require that the proposals they receive include proposed methodologies for evaluating the success of the proposed project and the degree to which it achieves its stated goals. Currently, many grantors are emphasizing that grant projects specify their objectives in terms of the expected outcomes and deliverables to benefit specific communities (see "Outcome-Based Evaluation Methodologies" below). Therefore, outcome-based project evaluation strategies that measure and report on the project's success (or failure) in meeting these goals are preferred. Grant-funding agencies want their grantees to focus on achieving project objectives. They appreciate confirmation that their grant funds were well spent. Including a project evaluation plan in your proposal is good marketing as well as good project management, even if it is not a mandatory stipulation.

Your project evaluation model and plan should answer these questions:

- What specific goals are you trying to achieve?
- What measurable milestones will you reach in meeting those goals?
- How will you know whether you are achieving your goals?
- How will your funder know that you are making progress toward your goals?
- What will you measure to evaluate your progress?

FIGURE 10.4

EXAMPLE OF A PROPOSED LOGICAL PROJECT TASK OUTLINE AND BUDGET

MILANOF-SCHOCK LIBRARY (MSL) SENIORS PROJECT TASKS AND BUDGET

Proposed Project Tasks	LSTA Funds Requested	Library Equivalent Funds	Totel Funding
TASK 1—Computer Course Development and Presentation			
1A. Hire outside instructors: 96 sessions × 2 Hrs. each @ $35/Hr.	$6,720		$6,720
1B. Acquire instructional texts and CDs for students: 960 @ $5		$4,800	$4,800
1C. Rent classroom: 96 sessions @ $25		$2,400	$2,400
TASK 2—Senior Website Development			
2A. Hire outside website designer: 24 Hrs. @ $35/Hr.	$840		$840
2B. Develop and maintain website: 8 Hrs. × 12 months @ $15		$1,440	$1,440
TASK 3—Laptops for Lending and Homebound Computer Access			
3A. Acquire ten large-screen laptop computers, software and modems @ $1800	$18,000		$18,000
3B. Hire and train field instructors: three instructors × 10 Hrs. × $10		$300	$300
TASK 4—Delivery of Library Materials and Laptops to Homebound Seniors			
4A. Develop homebound collection materials: 500 titles @ $20 (av.)	$1,000		$1,000
4B. Hire half-time senior/homebound coordinator: 1040 Hrs. @ $10	$10,400		$10,400
4C. Acquire laptop circulation computer		$1,600	$1,600
4D. Acquire homebound delivery vehicle (used)	$5,000		$5,000
4E. Maintain and fuel vehicle: 10,000 miles @ $.36	$3,600		$3,600
4F. Acquire vehicle internal shelving and book delivery carts		$500	$500

Proposed Project Tasks	LSTA Funds Requested	Library Equivalent Funds	Total Funding
4G. Volunteer and staff homebound labor: 1,000 Hrs. @ $8 (equiv.)		$8,000	$8,000
4H. Visit homebound: 4 Hrs./week × 52 @ $17		$3,536	$3,536
TASK 5—Evaluation			
5A. Design outside questionnaire: 24 Hrs. @ $50		$1,200	$1,200
5B. Analyze questionnaire responses: 36 Hrs. @ $50		$1,800	$1,800
5C. Prepare interim reports: 11 mo. reports @ 1Hr. × $16		$176	$176
5D. Prepare final report: 16 Hrs. @ $16		$256	$256
COST TOTALS:	**$45,560**	**$26,008**	**$71,568**

◆ What records and information will you keep to allow you to measure your progress?

◆ What data collection methods and tools will be employed?

◆ Will evaluations be objective and accurate, employing statistically valid methodology?

PROJECT EVALUATION METHODOLOGIES

In developing an evaluation plan, there are basically two types of project evaluation methods that can be considered: formal and informal.

Formal Evaluation Methodologies

Formal evaluations employ statistically rigorous methodologies and data collection instruments developed and applied by survey specialists and statisticians. This often involves random sampling of target populations, development of objective data-collection tools and survey instruments, and statistical analysis

FIGURE 10.5

EXAMPLE OF A PROPOSED LSTA PROJECT MILESTONE (GANTT) CHART

MSL Senior Project Schedule (Assuming 1/04 Start-up)

TASKS	J	F	M	A	M	J	J	A	S	O	N	D
Develop and refine new seniors courses												
Present courses												
Design seniors website												
Implement and maintain seniors website												
Implement computer outreach program for homebound												
Provide homebound seniors access to library materials												
Develop evaluation plan												
Administer questionnaires	▶	▶	▶	▶	▶	▶	▶	▶	▶	▶	▶	▶
Evaluate results												
Report to commonwealth libraries		▶	▶	▶	▶	▶		▶	▶	▶	▶	Final Rept.

of collected data to develop conclusions. In this technique, the respondent either completes a formal questionnaire or is interviewed using questions and recorded responses on a one-to-one basis. With a skilled questionnaire designer and an objective interviewer, these types of surveys can yield excellent results, but they can be very labor-intensive and require skilled questionnaire designers, interviewers, and statistical analysts. Most public libraries do not have these kinds of in-house resources and must rely on an outside organization to provide this expertise. If your granting agency requires this sort of formal evaluation for the project you are proposing, consider partnering with an academic institution in your area that may have a survey institute or statistical survey faculty that does this type of work. Another alternative is to team up with a local commercial survey or marketing firm that does product evaluation studies. Get these partners involved in the writing of your proposal's evaluation plan and cite them in your qualifications and management proposal sections. Try to get this support on a pro bono basis if you can, but if you must pay for it, include the cost of this consulting support in your project cost proposal. Many consultants may not charge for the help they provide on a proposal if they are promised a contract when the grant is funded. This is known as a "contingency agreement."

Informal Evaluation Methodologies

If the grantor allows for an informal evaluation methodology, you may be able to perform this with your in-house staff. Although these evaluations are not as statistically rigorous as formal evaluations, they can be objective and accurate if done right. I personally prefer informal interviews using focus interview/focus group techniques that I successfully employed for years in industry. Focus interviewing can be done either one-on-one or en masse as a focus group. The principles and outcomes are the same, but you get more depth in the one-on-one interviews.

Project evaluation by focus interviewing starts with a few broad-based questions such as:

- ◆ Why did you enroll in the computer course?
- ◆ What specific objective(s) did you want to achieve?
- ◆ Did you achieve your objective(s)?
- ◆ What did you like about the course?
- ◆ What did you not like about the course?
- ◆ What would you like included in future courses?

You can then pick up and focus on relevant aspects of the individual's or group's answers and ask them to elaborate or explain, maintaining a dialogue until you get the depth of information you need. For example:

- ◆ You said that the instructor went too fast—can you elaborate?
- ◆ You said that some students held the class back. In what way did they do this?
- ◆ What did you mean by the statement "the homework assignments were not relevant"?

Kruger and Richard's book *Focus Group: A Practical Guide for Applied Research* is a good guide to conducting focus group evaluations.

OUTCOME-BASED EVALUATION METHODOLOGIES

A primary source of federal grant funds for libraries in the United States are Library Service and Technology Act grants. Here federal monies are made available to the states by the federal Institute of Museum and Library Services. The Government Performance and Results Act of 1993 (see chapter 4) requires that federal agencies establish objective, quantifiable, and measurable performance goals and indicators for their programs. In response to this act, the IMLS has developed an outcome-based planning and evaluation model as a foundation of its grant making. Accordingly, those of us who request LSTA and other IMLS funds must include in their grant proposals project evaluation plans which employ outcome-based evaluation (OBE) methodologies. Grantsmen and grantswomen should therefore become familiar with this approach as outlined below.

The IMLS website (http://www.imls.gov/applicants/basics.shtm) defines outcome-based evaluation thus:

> How does a library or museum do outcome evaluation?
>
> Outcome-based evaluation defines a *program* as a series of services or activities that lead towards observable, intended changes for participants ("a Born to Read program increases the reading time caretakers spend with children"). Programs usually have a concrete beginning and a distinct end. The loan of a book or an exhibit visit might constitute a program, since these have a beginning and an end, and increased knowledge is often a goal. An individual might complete those programs in the course of a single visit. Outcome measurements may be taken as each individual or group completes a

set of services (a workshop series on art history, an after-school history field trip) or at the end of a project as a whole. Information about participants' relevant skill, knowledge, or other characteristic is usually collected at both the program beginning and end, so that changes will be evident. If a program wants to measure longer-term outcomes, of course, information can be collected long after the end of the program.

To use a familiar example, many libraries and museums provide information online. They could count the number of visitors to a web page, based on logs any Internet server can maintain. These numbers could indicate how large an audience was reached. Offering a resource, though, only provides opportunity. In order to know if online availability *had a benefit*, an institution needs to measure skills, attitudes, or other relevant phenomena among users and establish what portion of users were affected.

To capture information about these kinds of results, a library or museum could ask online visitors to complete a brief questionnaire. If a goal is to increase visitor knowledge about a particular institution's resources, a survey might ask questions like, "Can you name 5 sources for health information? Rate your knowledge from 1 (can't name any) to 5 (can name 5)." If visitors rate their knowledge at an average of 3 at the beginning of their experience, and 4 or 5 (or 2) at the end, the sponsoring institution could conclude that the web site made a difference in responders' confidence about this knowledge. It should be clear that such a strategy also lets you test your effectiveness in communicating the intended message!

It is rarely necessary to talk to every user or visitor. In many cases, and depending on the size of the target audience and the outcome being measured, a voluntary sample of users or visitors can be used to represent the whole with reasonable confidence. Most institutions find that people enjoy and value the opportunity to say what they think or feel about a service or a product.

As adopted by the IMLS, outcome-based evaluation methodology measures a grant project against six basic parameters:

1. Program purpose
2. Program services
3. Intended outcomes
4. Indicators
5. Data source(s)
6. Target for change

The following three sections provide examples of how outcome-based evaluation methodology was applied to three successful LSTA grant projects I won for my public library in 2004, 2007, and 2009, respectively, collectively yielding about $122,000 in grant awards.

LSTA Grant Program, Project A

Computer Tutor to the Technologically Handicapped and Reads on Wheels Homebound Delivery

1. *Program Purpose:* The Milanof-Schock Library provides computer instruction and homebound delivery to facilitate computer literacy and access to traditional library services for senior citizens and the handicapped in the five municipalities of its service area

2. *Program Services*
   a. Present a series of twelve senior-oriented computer courses from basic to advanced
   b. Development of a senior-oriented website
   c. Lending of laptop computers to seniors and the homebound
   d. Delivery of computer-based and traditional library services to the homebound

3. *Intended Outcomes*
   a. Technologically handicapped seniors will become computer-literate and improve their quality of life
   b. More seniors will be able to access computer-based library services
   c. Homebound residents will have access to the library's books, periodicals, audiovisual materials, and computer-based services

4. *Indicators*
   a. Number of seniors enrolling in library computer courses
   b. Number of seniors who employ computer-based library services
   c. Circulation of library materials to the homebound

5. *Data Source(s)*
   a. Entry and exit questionnaire surveys for students at beginning and end of each course series

    b. Interview survey of homebound delivery recipients

    c. Computer usage and circulation statistical analysis for target populations

6. *Target for Change*

    a. Students report 75 percent or more increase in comfort levels with computers from beginning to end of each four-week course

    b. Library computer usage by seniors increases by 100 percent

    c. Homebound delivery participants increase from 0 to 100 in three months

LSTA Program Grant, Project B

Multi-Media Language Learning Is Fun

1. *Program Purpose:* The Milanof-Schock Library facilitates foreign, English-language, and American Sign Language self-instruction for children, youth, and adults

2. *Program Services*

    a. Acquire and lend interactive, computer-based foreign language-learning kits (e.g., Rosetta Stone, etc.)

    b. Acquire and lend audio language-learning kits (e.g., Pimsleur, etc.)

    c. Acquire and lend interactive and audio English and American Sign Language language-learning kits (e.g., California Language Labs, etc.)

3. *Intended Outcomes*

    a. Children and youth will get a head start on foreign language instruction

    b. Children and youth will improve their grades in language classes

    c. School language programs will be supplemented by the library's offering of self-instruction in forty-seven foreign languages

    d. Foreign travelers will obtain basic language skills

    e. English as a second language students will accelerate their acquisition of English language skills

    f. Those desiring to improve communication with the hearing-impaired will master American Sign Language

4. *Indicators*

   a. Increased circulation of self-instructional language-learning kits

   b. Feedback on degree of satisfaction with language-learning materials via survey

5. *Data Source(s)*

   a. Questionnaire survey placed in all language kits to be completed and returned with kit

   b. Random focused interviews with patrons (and parents of children) returning borrowed language materials

   c. Focused interviews with elementary, middle, and high school language faculty and homeschool parents to determine positive impact of language kits on students who employed the kits

6. *Target for Change*: Foreign language and English as a second language proficiency and comfort level to increase 75 percent or more among participants

LSTA Grant Program, Project C

Improved Computer Instruction for All

1. *Program Purpose*: The Milanof-Schock Library provides computer-based earning for children, youth, seniors, and immigrants through courses and self-instruction in its computer learning laboratory

2. *Program Services*

   a. Provide ten modern, high-speed desktop instructional computers

   b. Provide ten modern, high-speed laptop instructional computers

   c. Provide appropriate classroom seating

   d. Provide appropriate auxiliary projection, audio, and printing hardware to support instruction

3. *Intended Outcomes*

   a. The quality of computer instruction and learning in the library will improve

   b. The enrollment in each computer course will double

   c. New software and instructional tools will be employed

4. *Indicators*

    a. Numerical increase in course enrollments by children, youth, seniors, and immigrants

    b. Improved satisfaction of computer course students and instructors

    c. Improved library patron computer skills

5. *Data Source(s)*

    a. Interview survey of students and instructors at course completion

    b. Course enrollment statistics

    c. Library use statistics for target groups

6. *Target for Change*: Participant satisfaction level with new hardware and software will be at least 75 percent positive

PRESENTING PROPOSED EVALUATION PLANS

More and more state grant-funding agencies (such as Pennsylvania Commonwealth Libraries) now require that LSTA grant proposals be submitted to them electronically (see chapter 11). These electronic submissions may require that grant requesters present their proposed OBE methodology in a tabular format in boxes contained in an online application form. An example of this type of submission is shown in figure 10.6 for a 2009 LSTA grant won by my library (the same one cited in the third example above). Note that the OBE parameters employed by local state agencies in their LSTA grant programs, such as those of Pennsylvania's Commonwealth Libraries, may vary somewhat from those specified by the IMLS.

More detail on outcome-based evaluation can be found in the 26-page manual *Perspectives on Outcome Based Evaluation for Libraries and Museums*, which is available online at www.imls.gov/pdf/pubobe.pdf or from the Institute of Museum and Library Services, 1800 M Street NW, 9th Floor, Washington, DC, 20036-5802; Phone: 202-653-4682; Fax: 202-653-4600.

MANAGEMENT PROPOSAL

Your proposal's project management section (often known as the management proposal) presents your planned schedule, staffing, and resources allocation (or the *When?* and *Whom?* of the proposed project's implementation).

FIGURE 10.6

EXAMPLE OF PROPOSED OUTCOME-BASED EVALUATION
PLAN IN TABULAR ONLINE SUBMISSION FORMAT
(FROM A 2009 LSTA GRANT PROPOSAL)

Goal	Data Source	Who	Intervals
1. Enable 100% more children and youth library users to more effectively access computer-based library educational programs	1. Statistical evaluation of course enrollment and retention	Program/course enrollees	1. At course registration 2. At course completion
1. Enable 100% more children and youth library users to more effectively access computer-based library educational programs	2. Anecdotal observation by instructors, proctors, and staff	1. Instructors 2. Proctors 3. Staff	At each course session
1. Enable 100% more children and youth library users to more effectively access computer-based library educational programs	3. Written questionnaires completed by students	Program/course enrollees	At course completion
1. Enable 100% more children and youth library users to more effectively access computer-based library educational programs	4. Focused interviews with students, instructor, and proctors	1. Students 2. Instructors 3. Proctors	At course completion
2. Enable 100% more senior library patrons to take improved computer-based courses in the library	1. Statistical evaluation of course enrollment and retention	Program/course enrollees	1. At course registration 2. At course completion
2. Enable 100% more senior library patrons to take improved computer-based courses in the library	2. Anecdotal observation by instructors, proctors, and staff	1. Instructors 2. Proctors 3. Staff	At each course session

Goal	Data Source	Who	Intervals
2. Enable 100% more senior library patrons to take improved computer-based courses in the library	3. Written questionnaires completed by students	Program/course enrollees	At course completion
2. Enable 100% more senior library patrons to take improved computer-based courses in the library	4. Focused interviews with students, instructor, and proctors	1. Course enrollees 2. Instructors 3. Proctors	At course completion
3. Improve effectiveness of ESL training for 100% of non-English-speaking patrons via computer instruction	1. Statistical evaluation of course enrollment and retention	Program/course enrollees	1. At course registration 2. At course completion
3. Improve effectiveness of ESL training for 100% of non-English-speaking patrons via computer instruction	2. Anecdotal observation by instructors, proctors, and staff	1. Instructors 2. Proctors 3. Staff	At each course session
3. Improve effectiveness of ESL training for 100% of non-English-speaking patrons via computer instruction	3. Written questionnaires completed by students	Program/course enrollees	At course completion
3. Improve effectiveness of ESL training for 100% of non-English-speaking patrons via computer instruction.	4. Focused interviews with students, instructor, and proctors	1. Course enrollees 2. Instructors 3. Proctors	At course completion

The management proposal should provide an explanation of how the project's resources and time will be managed and by whom to achieve the desired results. Among elements to be discussed here are scheduling, staffing, partnering, reporting, and the allocation of other non-staff resources. Describe any internal library management systems and policies you will employ to ensure effective project management, quality control, and achievement of expected results. The makeup of the proposed project team, its organization, and its leadership should be clearly stated here, with cross-references to staff biographies in the qualifications section or an appendix. Clearly state with whom you intend to partner and the partner's specific roles and skills. If you have a letter of commitment from the partner, reference it here and include it as an appendix.

PROJECT SCHEDULE

One important part of the project management section is the project schedule, which gives the *when* of your proposed project. A clear project schedule from project initiation to the final report should be included in this section. This can be presented either graphically as a Gantt chart, as shown in figure 10.5, or as a sequential list of steps with elapsed time or dates for each step, such as shown below.

GOAL 1: Meet with Latino community leaders to define and classify their community's needs and to increase their awareness of library services.

>   *Task 1:* Identify five to ten representative Latino community leaders
>> Elapsed time: two weeks
>> Completion date: June 1

>   *Task 2:* Schedule meetings with identified Latino leaders
>> Elapsed time: one week
>> Completion date: June 8

>   *Task 3:* Interview Latino leaders
>> Elapsed time: two weeks
>> Completion date: June 22

>   *Task 4:* Produce draft report of Latino community library needs
>> Elapsed time: three weeks
>> Completion date: July 14

Task 5: Review draft report with Latino community leaders and validate findings

    Elapsed time: two weeks

    Completion date: July 28

Task 6: Prepare and issue final report on Latino community needs

    Elapsed time: Two weeks

    Completion date: August 12

Total elapsed time to achieve goal: Twelve weeks

PROJECT REPORTING

The proposed project reporting schedule in your management proposal should include all scheduled project progress reports, financial reports, the final report, and any scheduled review meetings with the grantor. It should also provide a listing of all reports and meetings, with a brief narrative description of what each will cover. This is important because grantors like to be kept apprised of the progress of their grant projects and appreciate (and often require) the submission of regular monthly or quarterly progress and expense reports and a final report from the grantees. Some grantors may request periodic meetings or site visits to keep tabs on larger projects. You should also include these meetings in your schedule and narrative.

STAFFING PLAN

In the staffing portion of your management proposal, you specify *who* will do *what*. Include here the job descriptions and background statements of assigned staff, or the qualifications you will seek in staffing for the project. This is true even if "staff" will actually be outside contractors or volunteers.

It is advisable to include a functional (i.e., job title) project organization chart showing the project reporting hierarchy in the proposal. An example is shown in figure 10.7. It is customary to cite the names of key team members and job titles for support staff, with full-time equivalents shown for each staff grade category on the chart. Again, your narrative text should provide a functional description of each position on the chart. Some proposal writers prefer to list the job title and worker qualifications but not include the names of proposed team members in the proposal. This allows for flexibility in staffing when the project

FIGURE 10.7

SAMPLE FUNCTIONAL PROJECT STAFFING PLAN'S
ORGANIZATION CHART

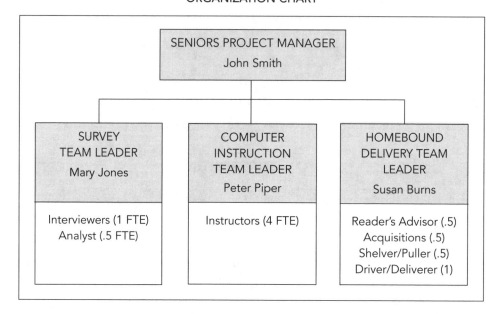

is finally funded and commences, which could be months after the proposal was written. If you do decide to include names (or are required to do so by the RFP), then qualify your staffing plan by including the statement "we reserve the option of substituting staff members with equivalent or better qualifications for those cited in the proposal." If you can, avoid key personnel clauses, which specify that only a specifically named individual may perform a certain project task. This locks you in contractually, and you may need a contract modification to substitute another individual if the "key person" is unavailable for any reason.

RESOURCE PLAN

Your proposed resource plan is part of your management proposal and is where you define the non-staff resources that will be required by the project and how they will be acquired, managed, and allocated. Include all significant resources to be acquired, such as facilities, furnishings, hardware, software, expendables, communications, and travel. The resource categories you discuss here should be the same ones you present in your cost proposal (see below). Be as specific as you can in defining the resources you will need, but do not lock yourself into

FIGURE 10.8

EXAMPLE OF A PROPOSED RESOURCE TABLE WITH OPTIONAL
ITEMIZED COST DATA (FROM A 2009 LSTA GRANT APPLICATION)

Budget Expenditure	Description	Amount/ Item	Quantity	Proposed Location
Desktop computer system with large-screen monitors	Lenovo MP 57P (or equivalent) with 22" screen	$2,000 each	10	Library computer lab
Laptop computer system	Lenovo T61 (or equivalent)	$1,200 each	10	Library computer lab and lent to students
Computer software	OS, MS Office, Adobe, etc.	$500 each	20	Library computer lab and lent to students
High-speed laser printer	HP CM1312nfi MFP (or equivalent)	$500 each	2	Library computer lab
Instructional projector	Optima HD72 (or equivalent)	$1,000	1	Library computer lab
Instructor classroom server	Dell PowerEdge 840 (or equivalent)	$2,400	1	Library computer lab
Computer lab renovation	New workstations, chairs, wiring, screens, etc.	$5,600	1	Library computer lab

specific branded products and models, because these may not be available (or better ones might be introduced) by the time the project is funded and kicks off. You can do this by citing a specific product and then using the phrase "or an equivalent" (e.g., "we will acquire a Lenovo G40 laptop computer *or an equivalent device*"). State the specific quantity of each resource item to be acquired such as number of pieces, square feet of space, reams of paper, and so on.

You can present your proposed resource requirements as a list or a table. I prefer the tabular format, which is easy for the reviewer to scan and is often required in electronic proposal submissions. Figure 10.8 contains an example of a resource table from a 2009 LSTA grant proposal; the cost column may not be required in the management proposal's resources section if you present these same data in the cost proposal. Compare this table with the one in figure 10.9, which gives more detailed cost information.

FIGURE 10.9

EXAMPLE OF A SPREADSHEET-FORMAT COST PROPOSAL
WITH ASSOCIATED NARRATIVE SHOWING MATCHING (IN-KIND)
FUNDING (FROM A 2009 ASSOCIATION GRANT APPLICATION)

15. A. Project Budget
Project Title: Marietta Community Library Outpost

Description	Cost /Unit	Units	Total
Personnel			
Administration and coordination (in-kind matching funds)	00.00/hr	144	$0.00
Outreach and marketing (in-kind matching funds)	00.00/hr	144	$0.00
Reference librarian	17.00/hr	2,016	$34,272.00
Subtotal			$34,272.00
Supplies, Material, and Equipment			
Computer hardware	$700	5	$3,500.00
Software	$300	5	$1,500.00
Laser printer	$500	1	$500.00
All-in-one fax/printer/scanner/copier	$230	1	$230.00
Wireless router	$400	1	$400.00
Cleaning service	$150/mo	18	$2,700.00
Supplies	$100/mo	18	$1,800.00
Internet connectivity	$175/mo	18	$3,150.00
Printing and publicity	$100/mo	18	$1,800.00
Electric	$100/mo	18	$1,800.00
Furniture		14 pcs.	$5,250.00
Mileage (library deliveries)	$.585/mile	5,040	$2,948.00
Subtotal			$25,578.00
Total			**$59,850.00**
Project in-Kind (if applicable)	$20.00/hr	288	$5,760.00

Narrative Budget Summary

Personnel

- Administration and coordination; Outreach and marketing staff time donated in-kind at no charge to project
- Reference librarian(s) to work at outpost 4 hours/day, 7 days/week

Supplies, Material, and Equipment (hardware and software acquired at government discount rate)

- Five Dell Inspiron 530 desktop computers with 17" monitors or equivalent; 4 for public, 1 for librarian
- Five XP Professional or Vista software suites or equivalent (final choice on advice of County IT Dept.)
- One HP CM1312 high-speed laser printer or equivalent for public computers
- One HP CB029A all-in-one fax/printer/copier/scanner or equivalent for librarian
- One Cisco 877 wireless router or equivalent
- Weekly facility cleaning and janitorial service
- Office supplies include expendables, with computer printing costs offset by nominal fees ($.15/page)
- DSL wide-band line to link computers to main library T1 line and provide telephone/fax service for librarian
- Printing: Instructional handouts, forms, and publicity flyers and posters
- Electric: 12,000 KW hours/year @ $.10 (includes HVAC)
- Furniture: 4 computer workstations @ $600; 1 reference librarian workstation @ $850; 1 study table with 4 chairs for $1,000; 4 bookshelves @ $250
- Mileage: Daily delivery of library materials to/from regional library to Marietta @ ten miles per round trip

COST PROPOSAL

Following the grant writer's rule number 6 (*Read the grantor's instructions and give them exactly what they want*), review the RFP to verify what grant project costs are allowable (e.g., overhead, staff labor, space, etc.) and how they are to be represented in your proposal. Once you know the rules, you can then develop your itemized cost proposal. This will present your proposed project's total expenses category by category. Do not forget to include any contribution your community is making to your project's budget by including matching funds (in both cash and kind) that will be provided by the library, its volunteers, and its partners. Many RFPs now require a statement of matching funds proposed by the grantee (see below).

In general, grant makers prefer to fund projects or special programs, not routine operations. Therefore, at least 80 percent of your proposal budget should be dedicated to the project or program you are proposing.

COST CATEGORIES

Typically, your cost proposal will require that you allocate your proposed project's task expenditures among expense categories. The usual set of budget categories found in a library grant project includes

capital costs (land, construction, etc.)

matching funds

project income

advertising and promotion

collection materials acquisition

communications

consultants, contractors, outside instructors

fees, licenses, taxes

furniture

hardware

labor (management, professional, and clerical)

overhead (including labor fringe benefits)

postage

printing

software

space

supplies

travel and living expenses

utilities

COST PROPOSAL FORMAT

Some RFPs require that the proposed grant budget be presented in a prescribed budget format (often using MS Excel). Figure 10.9 shows an example of a proposed library-oriented grant project budget presented in RFP-specified Excel spreadsheet format along with a narrative summary, which was also required by the RFP. Note that matching funds, in the form of in-kind labor, are also shown in this budget statement. Budget narratives may be included in the budget table or as footnotes or endnotes.

If a grantor does not specify a set cost-proposal format, you don't have to go out and hire a CPA or buy accounting software to present your proposed project budget. Use common sense to develop your own budget table that tells what funding you need in unambiguous and uncomplicated terms. I did this in two different LSTA grant proposals to the Pennsylvania Commonwealth Libraries, as illustrated in figures 10.4 and 10.10. It is best to present a complete project budget, with the cost projections matched to the project tasks and schedules cited in other proposal sections (using the same task names) and itemized by typical expenditure categories such as those cited above.

In developing your project budget, build it from the bottom up. First start with itemized unit costs (e.g., hourly labor rates, cost per book, cost per travel mile, cost per computer, etc.). Then, on a task-by-task basis, multiply each unit cost by the number of required units to get a cost total for the task (e.g., hours of labor, number of computers to be purchased, etc.). This will let the proposal reviewers see clearly how the total project cost was derived and will allow them to verify your costing bases and/or request a budget revision if they do not agree with the quantities or prices you cite (see "When a Grantor Requests Proposal or Budget Revisions" below).

LABOR COSTS

When presenting labor costs in a proposal, it is preferable to do so by labor class or job title (e.g., reference librarian, etc.) and to give the average or midpoint salary for the labor class rather than giving a specific individual's name and exact compensation. Provide the unit hourly cost and then multiply by the number of hours for the total. If permissible, you might want to use the *loaded* labor rate, which is direct compensation, plus an average hourly rate for employee fringe benefits (e.g., insurance, retirement, etc.). In calculating labor hours and costs vs. schedules, it is helpful to note that a standard forty-hour workweek translates into 2,080 person-hours per year. Take out holidays, vacations, and sick days and you get about 220 person-days or 1,776 productive person-hours per year. Divide your total hours by either of these numbers and you get the number of full-time equivalent person-years (or person-months if you multiply person-years by 12).

In preparing grant proposals which involve purchases of materiel, many not-for-profits request funding for materiel such as computers and library book collections but leave out the incremental labor costs that are necessary to acquire and install the items such as programming, acquisitions, cataloging, and so forth. Unless prohibited, consider including proposed project labor expense in your cost proposal. Even if you don't want to include these labor costs as part of the grant funds requested, you can include them as in-kind matching funds.

MATCHING FUNDS AND PROJECT INCOME

More and more grantors are requiring that prospective grantees include some level of matching funds in their proposal budgets. Some RFPs do not specify a specific amount of matching funds while others are very precise, requiring matches from 10 to 100 percent (i.e., dollar for dollar). Even if matching funds are not a mandatory requirement, it is good marketing to cite some level of matching to demonstrate that your institution has a serious commitment to the project and is willing to share the costs.

Though your institution may be cash poor, do not let a matching funds stipulation thwart your grant seeking. Unless prohibited, in most cases you can also consider as matching funds the dollarized actual or market value of your staff and volunteer labor, facilities space committed to the project, travel and living expenses, expendable materials, and overhead. You may also be allowed to consider fees or community sponsorships generated by a program as a form of matching funds. Grants, in-kind or cash, from other cooperative agencies may also be cited as matching funds. For example, my library holds an annual community bicycle-safety rodeo for about 300 kids which is funded by a grant from a local family foundation, plus in-kind "matching funds" provided by a local Kiwanis club (which provides refreshments and volunteer labor), a local Boy Scout troop (volunteer labor and tents), two local police departments (labor for safety instruction and crowd control), and a local investment firm that covers advertising costs and the printing of handouts. We dollarize these partner donations and list the total as *matching funds*.

In your cost proposal budget, clearly differentiate between funds requested from the grantor and matching funds from your library and its partners in the project budget. Examples of how to present matching funds in a proposed grant budget are found in figures 10.4, 10.9, and 10.10. In figure 10.4, the column labeled "LIBRARY EQUIVALENT FUNDS" presents the dollarized value of library staff and volunteer labor hours as equivalent matching funds. Figure 10.9 shows in-kind (i.e., pro bono) labor as matching funds, with the dollarized equivalent value given. In figure 10.10, the "Revised Budget" column shows total funds required broken down by those supplied by the grantor Commonwealth Libraries ("Comm. Libs.") and the grantee Milanof-Schock Library ("MSL").

PROPOSED BUDGET ACCURACY

Try to present as accurate an estimate of costs as possible and cite your price estimate sources (e.g., manufacturer's catalog, quote from a salesman, recent similar purchase, etc.) as appropriate. Most grantor reviewers and accountants understand that cost proposals are estimates and will accept ± 10 percent accuracy in a proposal budget. More budget detail is better than less, and it helps validate your cost estimate. Use whole dollars, and if a large amount of money is being requested, it is okay to round off costs to the nearest $10 or even $100. Cite brand names and model numbers for major equipment purchases (being sure to also state "or equivalent"). If you are quoting a price that may fluctuate based on market conditions, state this and give the date that you received the quote and state "subject to market fluctuations." Do not pad your budget by inflating prices. Competent reviewers know the cost of goods and services and understand prevailing wages. If a grantor believes that you are trying to deceive them in your proposed project budget, your chances of winning are nil and you can poison the waters for future grant opportunities.

WHEN A GRANTOR REQUESTS
PROPOSAL OR BUDGET REVISIONS

After reviewing a proposal, it is not unusual for a grantor to request revisions to your proposed project's plan or budget as a condition for further review or award. The revisions might include downscaling or eliminating certain tasks, reducing quantities on multiple cost items, changes to the pricing of certain items, inclusion of matching or shared costs, or the explanation and itemization

FIGURE 10.10

RESOURCE COST TABLE SHOWING A REVISED BUDGET
TO INCLUDE MATCHING FUNDS (FROM A 2009 LSTA GRANT PROPOSAL)

Budget Expenditure	Description	Unit Price	Quantity	Total Original Grant Cost	REVISED BUDGET Total	REVISED BUDGET Comm. Libs[1]	REVISED BUDGET MSL[2]
Desktop computer system with large-screen monitors	Lenovo MP 57P with 22" screen (or equivalent)	$2,000 each	10	$20,000	$20,000	$18,000	$2,000
Laptop computer system	Lenovo T61 (or equivalent)	$1,200 each	10	$12,000	$12,000	$10,000	$2,000
Computer software	e.g., MS XP, OS, MS Office, Adobe, etc.	$500 each	20	$10,000	$10,000	$6,000	$4,000
High-speed laser printer	HP CM1312nfi MFP (or equivalent)	$500 each	2	$1,000	$1,000	$500	$500
Instructional projector	Optima HD72 (or equivalent)	$1,000	1	$1,000	$1,000	$1,000	
Instructor classroom server	Dell PowerEdge 840 (or equivalent)	$2,400	1	$2,400	$2,400	$1,000	$1,400
Computer lab renovation	New workstations, chairs, wiring, screens, etc.	$5,600	1	$5,600	$5,600	$3,500	$2,100
			Total	$52,000	$52,000	$40,000	$12,000

1. Commonwealth Libraries = Grantor Funds
2. Milanof-Schock Library = Grantee Matching Funds

of certain collective costs. This, in my view, is usually a very good sign, which shows that the grantor is taking your proposal seriously and wants to work with you in making the project suitable for an award. Often, a grantor may like your proposal idea but cannot totally fund it as requested. They will work with you to reduce the projected costs to match their available grant funding. My philosophy here, again, is to be responsive and give the reviewers what they want, provided you do not jeopardize your project.

A note of caution should be added here. Let's say you have a situation where despite the fact that have carefully crafted your proposed project budget with little or no fat in it, a grant maker asks you to reduce the amount of your grant request. Be careful to advise the grant maker that cutting funds will require some corresponding scaling-down of project task effort and deliverables unless you can make up the difference with matching funds. If the grantor asks for a cost cut so large as to put the successful completion of the proposed project in question, then you must respectfully bring this to their attention and attempt to negotiate a suitable compromise. If not, you may have to withdraw, because you should never embark on a project that you know will fail due to insufficient funding.

Often, a grantor's request for a proposal revision will require resubmission of the affected portions of your application. If your original proposal contained budget and resource tables, you may be able to respond to the grantor's revision request by just modifying and resubmitting the tables. For example, the computer hardware grant budget shown in figure 10.10 illustrates how the original resource table shown in figure 10.8 was expanded and resubmitted as a revised budget presentation. This was in response to the grantor's request that we absorb 23 percent of the project's total cost by providing matching funds. The total projected project cost was $52,000. We made the budget revisions required by the state (i.e., by including $12,000 in matching funds), and the state library found the proposal acceptable and awarded my library a $40,000 grant.

REVIEWING THE PROPOSED BUDGET

It is useful to have a knowledgeable financial person review your cost proposal. This person could be your library's bookkeeper, treasurer, accountant, or a volunteer familiar with not-for-profit or government budget categories and guidelines. If you are including indirect overhead costs in your proposal budget, it is essential that your accountant confirm that you are employing the proper and current fringe and shared administrative indirect rates and including all allowable expenses. For example, on some grants you can include the dollar-value pro rata operating expense for the portion of your facilities employed by the project as a valid overhead charge.

ENSURING SUSTAINABILITY

Grant makers generally want the projects they fund to serve as the foundations of ongoing, productive community services. Therefore, if your proposed project is not finite, they want you to give them some assurance that the effort will continue after the grant funding is spent. As a result, one finds that more and more grant providers now ask that your proposal provide a "sustainability" statement on how you will continue to fund the project after the grant monies are expended. This commitment to sustainable funding is usually included as part of the cost proposal. Here you may be required to specify future sources and amounts of funding for up to five years. In doing this, it is better not to rely on only "soft" sources such as future competitive grants or donations from the community. Try to provide "hard" assurances of sustainability such as fee-generated income, line-item government funding, or an endowment gift. Indicating that you will ensure sustainability by seeking additional grants is not convincing, and grantors seldom fund the same project twice.

QUALIFICATIONS STATEMENT

The qualifications statement is the overt selling portion of your proposal (as opposed to the subtle selling in the rest of the application). Here you must demonstrate your organization's ability to successfully conduct and conclude the proposed project. The statement is designed to tell the granting agency why they should award the grant to your library as well as to inspire confidence in your ability to successfully complete the proposed project. Put another way, here is where you convince the reviewer that he will never regret awarding a grant to you.

Put modesty aside here and clearly (but tastefully) cite the personal qualifications and relevant experience of your project team and the corporate strengths of your institution. Start by citing your institution's mission and relevant history, including related programs, recognitions, and awards. Demonstrate your importance to your community and their acknowledgment of your contributions. Cite any community leaders who serve on your board and in your volunteer groups.

Be sure to showcase the qualifications of the project team leader (sometimes called the "principal investigator") and task leaders as they relate to the project.

In this section make reference to project team resumes, letters of commendation or recommendation, favorable articles, and awards that are contained in the proposal's appendixes. Cite any similar successful efforts that the library may have conducted. If any of your board members, library Friends, or volunteers have personal qualifications or affiliations relevant to the project, cite them as project advisors (with their permission, of course).

Do not neglect to cite the qualifications of any partners who will contribute to the project such as consultants, educators, associations, or government officials and include their resumes, awards, and letters of commitment in an appendix as well. Modesty is a false virtue in competitive grant seeking because grantors prefer to donate funds to winners who will use their money well. Convince them you are a winner. Do not be coy about stating your institution's qualifications to successfully conduct the project and why it deserves the grant. This is the time and place to cite any institutional awards or recognition you have received relative to the proposed project. It is also quite acceptable to solicit letters of recommendation from government officials, library system officials, and other luminaries and include them if this will support your request.

If space and the RFP allow, you may also wish to cite and include in the appendix favorable news clippings or feature articles from the media which reflect positively on your institution. Grant makers appreciate good publicity and tend to favor grantees that are in the limelight and get positive media recognition. For example, when my library included a group of positive news clippings in a grant application, the lead reviewer remarked to me (after award) that he was impressed by "all the ink your library had received in the local press." This will also demonstrate your library's ability to garner positive media coverage for the proposed project (see "Promotion Plan" below).

If the RFP cites the criteria that the grant maker will apply in screening proposals and selecting grantees, then it is good marketing to separately state each criterion, followed by an explanation of how your proposed project will meet the standard. For example, a recent RFP I received listed "Community Involvement" as a project criterion with a review score value of 35 percent. I responded to this in the qualifications section by listing each specific segment of the community that would participate in and benefit from the proposed project, as well as those that had contributed to the proposal effort.

By showing the proposal reviewers how well your application satisfies their award criteria, you are both helping them in their evaluation and also helping yourself to achieve a higher score.

The qualifications section is also where you affirm your institution's eligibility for the grant. Verify that your organization can comply with all compliance statements required by the funder on such things as antidiscrimination policies, privacy, fair labor practices, 501(c)(3) status, and so on.

Grant agencies want to be reasonably sure that they are investing in successful projects that will yield productive results, not in potential failures. This does not mean that you must guarantee in advance that each and every project you propose will be 100 percent successful. If there is an element of risk involved in your proposed project (and there almost always is some), identify it and directly address the steps you will take to minimize the chance of failure and maximize the probability of success. For example, if you are requesting funding for a teen reading program, you can recognize that it is difficult to attract youth to the library in today's world. In your proposal you can then cite this risk and how you will minimize it by proposing measures such as outreach to youth groups and partnerships with school reading counselors.

PROMOTION PLAN

Although supporting good works may be the primary objective of granting institutions, virtually all of them appreciate some good publicity. Therefore, include a section in your proposal on how you plan to publicize the proposed project and its results. Cite how you will use effective public relations techniques to make the media and public aware of the grant project and to attract the community's participation. It is good protocol in the proposal to offer to have the granting agency review in advance any press releases or other pieces of literature that will cite the agency's name or the project. It can be useful to also cite the public relations techniques you plan to employ to publicize the project. Public relations techniques that I cite in proposals and use to promote grant projects include

- ◆ press releases
- ◆ feature articles (in newspapers)
- ◆ the library column (in a newspaper)
- ◆ community bulletin boards
- ◆ library and other websites
- ◆ library and community newsletters
- ◆ flyers and brochures
- ◆ posters, signs, and banners
- ◆ talks at meetings

Library-oriented guidelines on how to prepare each of these types of promotional pieces can be found in my earlier book, *The Small Public Library Survival Guide*, published in 2008.

APPENDIXES AND ATTACHMENTS

If the RFP's specifications allow, use appendixes to the grant proposal to include any supplemental information that will help to strengthen your case, provide backup data to your proposal, and validate your stated need and your proposed solution. This can include resumes of the principal investigator and project staff, library organization charts, board rosters, letters of commitment from partners, letters of support from legislators, local officials, and community leaders, sample forms and survey questionnaires, statistical tables, examples of the library's prior relevant experience, awards and honors, press clippings, and the like. For example, in an LSTA grant proposal to the state requesting funds for a project to aid seniors, we included in the appendix newspaper clippings citing our library's prior program activities aimed at this target group.

An appendix is also a good place for any RFP-specified support documents and data such as audited financial statements, tax exemption certificates, your strategic plan, articles of incorporation, letters of recommendation, census statistics, and so on.

However, I must provide a few words of caution here. Do not use the attachments for information that is required in the body of the application. Be sure to cross-reference all supporting attachments to the appropriate text in the main proposal. Insert the attachments in the order indicated in the RFP. Do not overdo your appendixes and pack them with marginal information. Include in the appendix only what is necessary to prove your case or what is required by the RFP. Loading an appendix with too much irrelevant or superfluous information may have a negative impact on reviewers who will not be pleased if they have to sort through a lot of unessential detail.

Proposal Assembly, Editing, Review, and Submission

Kevin Wiberg, a development director for a large social service organization, advises that the proposal manager must be totally in charge of the final proposal steps when he states: "As team leader, your job is to review and incorporate all edits, so you should reserve control over the final product."[1] The proposal manager, therefore, must collect all the sections of the proposal from the writers, make sure they are complete, and assemble them in proper order and consistent format into the final proposal package.

This editorial review must ensure that the tone of the proposal and its terminology are consistent throughout all sections, especially if different people have written these. Check for numerical or programmatic inconsistencies. For example, if the person who wrote the staffing section decided to add a new position, both the project's design and the budget must reflect this change.

In addition to a content-oriented review, the proposal package should undergo an editorial review of its structure, grammar, punctuation, and spelling. Both computer and human spelling and grammar checkers should be employed. Here is where you need good proofreaders who may be more helpful if they have not been involved earlier.

This, however, does not preclude the proposal manager from asking someone unfamiliar with the proposed project to review the package to determine if it is clear and makes sense. Then, as a fail-safe, have someone familiar with the

RFP and your library's needs review the application to see if it has covered all points or if anything has been omitted.

Pay attention to your reviewers' questions and advice and modify your proposal to respond to their reactions.

ASSEMBLING THE PROPOSAL

Be sure to put together the proposal package exactly as specified in the RFP. It is useful to develop and apply a "grant submission checklist" such as that recommended by Gerding and MacKellar to ensure that you have paid attention to the important concerns.[2] Among the items on their checklist are these critical formatting factors:

- ♦ We have followed the instructions and guidelines of the funder's specifications.
- ♦ Our proposal meets page/word limits.
- ♦ The font type and size are correct.
- ♦ The margin size is correct.
- ♦ The line spacing is correct.
- ♦ We have used the specified type of paper.
- ♦ We did not bind unless we were told we could.
- ♦ The correct number of copies and the original were sent and we also retained a copy.
- ♦ We have included letters of support.
- ♦ We have the specified signatures.
- ♦ The proposal's introductory components are titled and compiled in the order specified:

  title sheet

  cover letter

  table of contents

  proposal summary
- ♦ Letters of agreement from partners are included.
- ♦ The proposal looks professional.

Make sure that all grant application information is submitted at the same time. Most grantor agencies will not consider additional information or materials submitted after your initial submission. For hard-copy submissions, use only the page format and binding method specified in the RFP. Number all your pages. If no binding type is indicated, do not put your completed application in ring binders, spiral binders, or in special packaging of any kind. This will create extra work for reviewers. I prefer using spring-type binder paper clips instead of staples because they allow reviewers to easily take the proposal apart and duplicate it as they may wish. You may want to consider tabs to make it easier for reviewers to quickly find the various sections. You may also use pocket folders, placing the proposal on one side and attachments on the other side.

FINAL REVIEW

Just prior to proposal submission, the proposal manager should give the complete, assembled proposal package a thorough final review. Take the time to double-check each section of the final proposal against the funder's instructions and review criteria. This review should address the following concerns and questions:

◆ Read over the application against the proposal instructions again.
◆ Did we miss anything?
◆ Have we answered all questions asked?
◆ Pay special attention to the criteria that will be used to judge the grant applications. Have you addressed those criteria?
◆ Are our physical page specifications correct throughout?
◆ Have we complied with RFP page and word count limits?
◆ Double-check that we have all the items on the RFP checklist.
◆ Have all required forms been completed and signed by the proper person?
◆ Have all required attachments been included?
◆ Is the package format in compliance with instructions?
◆ Is the delivery address correct?

Make sure you have the right number of copies required. Don't forget to make a complete copy for your library's file and copies for any partners or municipal, county, or state agencies that may be involved in the grant chain of submission or command. For example, in Pennsylvania, LSTA grants require that independent libraries submit proposals to the state through either a county district's or library system's administrators, and these entities will each require their own file copy of the proposal. Also, certain state construction grant applications have to be submitted through the library's home municipality, and they too will require a file copy.

PROPOSAL DELIVERY

In preparing your grant application proposal package for delivery, apply the cardinal grant seekers' rule number 6: *Read the grantor's instructions and give them exactly what they want.* Put the package together and address it exactly as specified. If a specific mode of delivery is named (e.g., USPS Express Mail or online submission, which is becoming more popular), then you must use it.

Then you must adhere to my rule number 7: *Always meet your submission deadline.* To paraphrase the poet Robert Burns, time, tide and *proposal deadlines* wait for no man. To illustrate this, note this last sentence in a 2009 Pennsylvania state grant RFP (emphasis mine):

> An original and four copies of the complete grant application, with all attachments and enclosures, must be received at the Office of Commonwealth Libraries by 5:00 p.m., June 30, 2009. We do not consider postmarks. Please allow sufficient time for applications to clear Commonwealth mail security. *Late applications will not be reviewed.*

Comply with the RFP submission schedule and delivery requirements religiously. Even though you may have written the world's best proposal, if you deliver it after the RFP-stated receipt (not mailing) deadline, then most likely your proposal will not be accepted or read and all your effort will have been for naught. If the RFP specifies that proposals must be received by 5:00 p.m. on a certain date, submitting it at 5:05 will likely mean that it will not be accepted or considered. With more and more agencies going to electronic submission of grants, it is important to get confirmation that your grant application was electronically delivered on time. Therefore, it is appropriate to ask that the grant receiver confirm the receipt of your e-proposal by return e-mail.

You can ensure on-time delivery by a foolproof method with confirmed delivery such as USPS Certified Mail with return receipt requested, USPS Registered Mail, USPS Priority Mail with delivery confirmation, USPS Priority Mail with signature confirmation, or USPS Express Mail.

If the grantor agency is not too far away, then hand-deliver the proposal yourself or via a trusted courier early on the due date (to allow for exigencies). Whatever delivery method you employ, also make sure that you obtain a dated receipt confirming delivery.

ELECTRONIC PROPOSAL SUBMISSION

More and more grantors are now distributing their RFPs electronically and specifying that, in turn, proposals to them be submitted electronically via online transmission as either attachments to e-mail or by special-purpose systems such as the Commonwealth of Pennsylvania's eGrant System, which employs pre-formatted proposal templates. Therefore, a grantsman will need the proper e-tools and know-how to do this. For example, to submit a federal grant application through Grants.gov, you will need to have Adobe Reader software on your computer to allow you to attach the required documents to your e-mail.

If submitting your proposal online or via another electronic format, certain precautions can save you time and ensure your proposal's acceptability. Most e-proposal templates impose limits on the maximum number of typed characters or words permitted in each section. In addition, most templates do not include spelling or grammar checkers. Therefore, to ensure compliance with word limits and to avoid typographical errors in your proposal, use the simple expedient of writing each proposal section first as an MS Word page, run it through the spell and grammar checkers, and then do a word or character count (found under the "Tools" heading on the toolbar) before copying it and dropping it into the e-proposal template. Also, check to ensure that all electronic attachments are included before sending the application forward. To aid in this, some e-proposal application templates have an "Add Attachment" feature, which lets you browse your computer's files and select the documents to be attached.

The MS Word draft proposal pages should also be saved as backup copies of your proposal because some of the special-purpose proposal templates do not have a save feature. It is a good precaution to make sure that all applications to be submitted electronically are first printed out, proofread, and checked to make sure everything required is included *before* you click on "Send."

If sending your electronic proposal as an attachment to an e-mail, structure the transmittal e-mail as you would if it were a hard-copy cover letter such as that in figure 10.1. Finally, in all electronic proposal submissions, I always ask the addressee to confirm that the proposal was properly received before the deadline so I can resend it if necessary. This can be done via a request in your e-mail cover letter or by a brief follow-up telephone call.

NOTES

1. Kevin Wiberg, "Leading a Proposal Development Team," *Centered* (newsletter of the Grantsmanship Center) 2, no. 7 (July 1, 2009).

2. Stephanie K. Gerding and Pamela H. MacKellar, *Grants for Libraries* (New York: Neal-Schuman, 2006), 142.

Post-proposal, Pre-award Marketing

Well, you have delivered your proposal to the grant agency. Although you might now wish to sit back and await the notice of grant award, there are still a few post-proposal marketing activities to be addressed.

FOLLOW-UP COMMUNICATION

In proposal follow-up communication, one should remember my rule number 8 of grantsmanship: *Don't be a pest.* Unnecessary inquiries are not appreciated by granting agencies. However, there are circumstances where continued contact after proposal submission is justified or required.

Confirmation of Delivery

It is acceptable to contact the grant agency to confirm that they have received your proposal if they have not automatically sent a receipt. You may do this by e-mail or telephone.

Status Inquiries

For the most part, experienced grantors will keep grant seekers up-to-date on the status of their submission's review process. One should therefore be patient and wait for the feedback notices to be received. Do not make any status inquiries prior to the specified grant award date. However, if the RFP-specified date for award has passed and you have received no notification, it would be appropriate to contact the grantor and politely inquire about the status of your proposal's review.

Advising the Grantor of Changes

It is considered good business ethics to advise the grantor of any major changes within your organization that might impact your proposal or project during their review of your proposal. Examples of these could be changes in proposed project staffing, reorganizations, changes in community needs, financial exigencies, changes to partners, and so on.

SITE VISITS AND ORAL INTERVIEWS

Some granting agencies may request that one or more of their reviewing officers be allowed to visit and inspect your library as part of a pre-grant review. I have experienced this when requesting funds from local foundations for facilities improvement. Other grantors may request a meeting where they will ask you to review your submission and respond to questions. Advice on how to handle these situations is given below.

Preparing a Grantor Site Visit

If a prospective grantor requests a site visit to your facility, here is how your organization can make a good impression. Pamela Grow provides these "Eight Tips to Prep for a Foundation Site Visit":[1]

- Make sure you understand what the foundation wants from the visit.
- Schedule the appointment for the best possible date and time for your organization.

♦ Arrange to have several board members and key staff present at the visit.

♦ Be sure the grantor knows where your institution is located and how to get there.

♦ Reconfirm the appointment the day before the visit.

♦ Be sure to have people from the constituency you serve available during the visit.

♦ Don't share only your success stories with your visitors; discuss some of the problems you're facing as well.

♦ Relax! Don't stress out during the visit; just be yourself.

Strategic scheduling of a site visit by a prospective grantor is something you should also consider. You can suggest a time when your library is usually full of a cross-section of patrons to demonstrate your service to all of the community, or a time when you have a popular kids' program to emphasize service to children. For example, a local community foundation requested a site visit at my library in connection with a grant request for additional shelving for our children's area. I scheduled the site visit to coincide with a very popular *Curious George* children's program. The foundation official was so impressed by our full parking lot and the scores of kids flowing out of our community room that he orally approved our grant during the visit.

Pre-award (Oral) Interviews

As an alternative to a site visit, a granting agency may invite the prospective grantee in for an interview or to make a presentation. This practice is common in competitive commercial contract situations and is sometimes employed by foundation grantors to help them select among the finalists in a close competition. In the contract game we called these "oral interviews," or "orals" for short. Grantors employ the oral to help them come to a final decision among two or three high scorers or, in a noncompetitive high-stakes award, to confirm that your organization is truly worthy. As with the site visit, you will not be invited to an oral interview unless you have satisfied the preliminary requirements for a grant and are a finalist. Now the grantor wants to meet the key players, discuss your proposed project and its budget with you, and learn more about your library to help decide if the grant should go to you or another. The grant interview, in many respects, is like a job interview where you need to sell yourself and your library and, in general, make a good impression.

When invited to an oral interview, here are some suggested guidelines for you to follow:

Verify the date, time, duration, and place of the interview and confirm it by letter or e-mail.

Politely ask if the interview will address any specific issues and if the grantor would like you to bring any backup data, provide handouts, make an overview presentation on the proposed project, and if so, the mode of presentation (e.g., slides, handouts, etc.). Ask how many copies of handouts are desired.

Ask who and how many people from your institution may attend, and adhere to the grantor's rules. Suggested attendees are your proposal manager, your proposed project manager (if different from proposal manager), and the library director or library board president. If budgets are an issue, bring a financial person.

All your attendees should be thoroughly familiar with the proposal and proposed project, and each should be provided with a copy of the proposal and any handouts. Your designated team leader should be prepared to present an executive summary of the proposed project in case one is requested at the meeting. Use the "iceberg approach," giving an overview summary and then providing below-the-surface details in response to questions.

Be prepared for questions from the grantor on any aspect of your proposal, project, or institution, including technical approach, budget, management, staffing, schedule, and so on.

Dress as you would for a job interview.

Designate one of your team to be the leader who will introduce your library's representatives, make any presentations, and either answer the grantor's questions or refer the question to another team member.

When asked questions by the grantor's representatives, politely respond as if the asker has not read your proposal. Avoid jargon and do not say, "If you had read the proposal you would already know this" or answer "Well, that's in the proposal," as this might offend the reviewers.

Keep to the grantor's meeting schedule and do not overstay your time allocation. When the interview seems to be nearing its end, ask if the grantor has any further questions and if there are any aspects of your proposal or proposed project that concern them. It is best to get any negative issues on the table so you can address and ameliorate them before you leave.

Finally, before you leave it is okay to politely ask what the next steps in the granting process will be.

LOSS DEBRIEFING

If, alas, your grant request is rejected, do not become depressed or angry. Remember that even the best of proposal writers seldom do better than winning one out of three grants. I would venture that the national average may be closer to one in ten. You can turn even a lost grant exercise into a learning experience. You do this by requesting a rejection debriefing. This is a normal procedure which most experienced grantor foundations, and even some government agencies, will usually agree to. The purpose of this debriefing is to respectfully request an explanation of why you did not receive an award and, specifically, to learn the weaknesses in your proposal and project plans. You will learn from this how to upgrade your future grant seeking to achieve success, and if you handle these communications with the grantor well (being respectful, eager to learn, and not defensive or angry), you may even be invited to resubmit your proposal with the suggested improvements and eventually take home a grant.

On the other hand, your rejection debriefing might determine that you were not awarded the grant because something about your organization or its proposed project was incompatible with the grantor's mission or scope of support. If the issue is a fundamental matter that cannot be resolved in future proposals, then you may decide it is better not to submit any future applications to this grantor so as not to waste their (and your) time. Hence, my rule number 10: *Do not continue to pursue lost causes.* As an example, my library won a grant on its first submission to a local community foundation. However, we were not successful on a second submission and requested a debriefing. We learned that the foundation had refocused its giving to supporting museums and those engaged in the arts. As a result, we no longer submit grant applications to them.

You may even consider asking for an informal proposal evaluation debriefing from grantors on your successful bids. I regularly did this when I wrote proposals for government, commercial, and other contract projects because it helps you perfect your style and gives some insight into the reviewers' psyche. It also establishes a rapport, which may aid in conducting your project as well as in subsequent grant pursuits with this grantor.

NOTE

1. Pamela Grow, "Eight Tips to Prep for a Foundation Site Visit," CharityChannel, June 3, 2009, www.charitychannel.com.

Contract Award and
Project Management

Congratulations! You have been notified that you have been awarded the grant. You are now a grantsman! Thank the funding agency. Express felicitations to your proposal team and partners! Have a little celebration! Now what?

As a first step, you should receive a letter and contractual documentation from the grantor confirming the grant award, its amount, and any terms and conditions that must be satisfied. For a small grant from a small local foundation, this can be as simple as a one-page letter with a check attached. However, for a large government grant (e.g., LSTA), the award document can be a multi-paged contract with attached reporting forms, schedules, legal stipulations, and signature pages which must be executed by officials of your institution, cooperating agencies, and the grantor. Some government contracts may also require statements of compliance and certifications to be executed for things like non-discrimination, fair employment practices, environmental concerns, and so on. Review these carefully as you would any contract because they are legally binding documents. Consult with your library's legal counsel as required. Review payment and reporting schedules and negotiate with the funder any changes you may require, and verify these by written amendments. (More on this is discussed below under "The Project Kickoff Meeting.")

PAYMENT SCHEDULES

Grant payment schedules may vary from grantor to grantor and also with the amount and duration of the grant. A small grant from a small foundation may involve a single lump sum payment at the time of award. However, large grants from large foundations or government agencies may involve installment payments or payments made upon the achievement of specific milestones, known as "progress payments" or "incentive payments." Therefore, you may find that a particular grant project requires that your institution will have to expend project funds prior to their reimbursement by the grantor. To avoid cash flow problems, review the grantor's payment schedule vs. the project's needs for cash with your financial officer before you begin the project. By doing this, the financial officer can set aside funds to cover project expenses until the grantor's checks start arriving. Even if a grantor has a fixed payment schedule, they may provide flexible payments in the event you need some seed-money cash at the beginning of the project, or they may increase the amount of an interim progress payment to help you bridge a cash flow gap. For example, I had a grant project where I had to purchase about $40,000 worth of computer hardware in the first few months of the project. Because of my heads-up to my library's treasurer, she was able to cash in some low-interest short-term securities to temporarily cover this big expense until the grantor's monthly payments reimbursed us. The treasurer and I both decided that this approach was preferable to completing, submitting, and negotiating a sheaf of government forms requesting an accelerated grant payment schedule.

Once you and the funder have agreed on the contract document, then you should adhere to rule number 9: *Follow the grant contract rules.* Adhering to this dictum will make relations with the grantor much more pleasant and will also label you as a cooperative and preferred grantee in the eyes of the funding agency. This is a positive reference for any future grant requests to this benefactor. If any of the rules aren't clear, then ask for clarification at the grant project kickoff.

It also definitely does not hurt to sincerely express your institution's gratitude to the grantor for the award as soon as you receive notification.

THE PROJECT KICKOFF MEETING

At the time of award, a granting organization may call for a meeting with a grantee to discuss grant initiation. In the contracting game we called this the "kickoff meeting." This meeting is a good place to resolve any questions you may have regarding the conduct and terms of the grant, and you, as grantee, may want to request a meeting if you have any outstanding questions or concerns about the project.

Whether you and the grantor hold a kickoff meeting or not, you will very likely have a number of questions and points of clarification regarding your grant. Make sure that these issues are resolved whether face to face, by telephone, e-mail, fax, or correspondence before you begin to work on the grant and expend any funds. Examples of typical grant start-up questions, if not covered in a contract document, are

- When can project work commence (i.e., when can we start spending grant monies)?
- Confirmation of the project's duration, milestones, and timetable.
- What are the reporting requirements?
- How and when will payments be made?
- Are there any restrictions on the use of grant funds (e.g., can they be applied to operating costs)?
- How must you account for expended funds?
- Will advance approval be required for certain expenses?
- Who are the points of contact?
- How is project publicity to be handled?
- How will changes of scope or budgetary reallocation be approved if necessary?

Once the administrative questions have been answered you are ready to roll. You can assemble your project team and give them their marching orders (including the final approved timetable and budget). Make sure the project director knows which tasks must begin immediately (e.g., hiring or assigning staff, acquiring space, etc.) and is fully aware of reporting and deliverable requirements. Touch base with all the departments in your organization that may be involved with the project, such as accounting, human resources, information technology, and so on, and advise them of what they are expected to contribute to the grant project effort; be sure to also clear all this with your library's executive director or board president.

GRANT AWARD AND PROJECT PUBLICITY

In her introduction to *The Big Book of Library Grant Money 2006*, ALA Development Office director Susan Roman gives good advice on publicizing your grant when she states:[1]

> Be sure to utilize as many publicity avenues as you have available. Remember public service announcements and the new opportunities that the Web provides. Recognizing the support of your donors is a wonderful tool in building long-term relationships. There are many ways to acknowledge your donors while getting the most out of public relations opportunities for your library and library initiatives. Check with your funder for specific guidelines on press releases.

A listing of specific publicity tools you can consider in advertising your new grant project can be found in chapter 10 in the section on the proposal's promotion plan.

PROJECT REPORTING

The grantor's contract document will usually specify your grantee reporting requirements. Typically these will be periodic monthly to quarterly financial and narrative progress reports, with a summary final report. Interim reports may discuss progress on each of the project's tasks, successes, and problems encountered, with attempted solutions and funds expended during the reporting period. Project evaluation is usually reserved for the final report. In some cases, a grantor representative may visit your library at the end of the project to review project results on-site in connection with the final report.

It is always a good idea to cite any favorable publicity received by the project in your progress reports, and relevant press clippings may be included as attachments. My library's first LSTA project providing homebound delivery service was highlighted on a local TV station's evening news broadcast. I included a video clip of the program slot that mentioned us in with my first quarterly report. The state library was so delighted with the positive publicity that they asked for extra video copies to be sent to the IMLS and their congressional oversight committees in Washington.

Project reports are good places to officially request project budget or scope modifications if required. For example, on large government-funded projects, it is sometimes necessary to move budget-allocated funds from one task (which may be underspent) to another task which requires additional support. I have done this a few times and used the quarterly reports to the state as the vehicle, attaching the necessary budget revision forms designed for this purpose.

If a delivery date for the final report is not specified, the report normally should be submitted within thirty days of grant completion. The final report should be a summary of the complete grant project and should also evaluate the success of the project in achieving its stated objectives in accord with the established evaluation criteria. The report should also provide a final financial accounting of all monies spent on the project, including both grantor and matching funds. Some government funding agencies may even request that an inventory of all equipment purchased with grant monies also be included in the final report, so save all your project purchase receipts and delivery invoices.

It is usually acceptable to include supporting attachments to the final report such as press releases, clippings, project event programs, project publications produced, and lists of library materials funded by the grant monies. Remember that it is good form (and sometimes mandatory) to identify or label all activities, publications, and equipment supported or purchased with grant funds with a statement such as "purchased with (or supported by) a grant from the XYZ Foundation."

On occasion, a grantor may request a site visit to observe project activities in person. This is most commonly done toward the end of the project. I suggest applying the guidelines presented in chapter 12 for a pre-award grantor site visit to those of a post-award site visit.

If the grantor specifies no final report format, you can craft your own. This is what I did in creating the final grant report to the Bill & Melinda Gates Foundation, which is shown in appendix B as a sample.

ENSURING PROJECT SUSTAINABILITY

It is important that worthwhile grant projects of importance to the community continue to provide benefits after grant funding is expended. Therefore, prior to the conclusion of the grant-funded phase of the project, a conscientious effort should be made to secure funding to sustain the efforts for as long as the need exists. Sustainability funding can come from a variety of sources, including allocation of internal funds via a budgeted line item, fee-based services, government appropriations, benefit events, or additional grant monies. It is good marketing and courtesy to report your sustainability plans and results to the grantors via the periodic and final reports, because they have a vested interest in seeing their good works continue.

NOTE

1. *The Big Book of Library Grant Money 2006* (Chicago: American Library Association, 2006), vii.

Writing a Request
for Proposal

Although this book is written for grant seekers, occasionally a library or other entity may be called upon to prepare and issue an RFP to solicit proposals for either a grant or a contract. This chapter will therefore provide guidance on the preparation of the reciprocal of the proposal: the request for proposal, or RFP.

There are useful guides available on how to prepare an RFP (such as the kits available from Technology Evaluation Centers, http://rfptemplates.technology evaluation.com). However, I find that virtually all of these are oriented toward writing RFPs to solicit bids on commercial contracts, not to request grant proposals from not-for-profit institutions, and there is a difference. Grant projects differ from typical client/contractor projects in that a grant project's purpose is to solicit proposals from libraries for projects to benefit the library patrons and community the grantee serves. The grant project idea is developed by the grant applicant within a grantor's broad mission area and funding parameters. On the other hand, in a *contractor* project, the RFP issuer specifies the project's parameters and the winning contractor is usually the low bidder, who will then conduct the project for the benefit of a specific client. An RFP that seeks a contractor to perform predefined, specific tasks is fairly detailed on project specifications and limits. However, in a grant RFP, the grantor usually presents broad mission-oriented goals and relies on grant applicants to submit proposals defining specific projects to achieve these goals. The comments below, therefore, will focus on writing effective RFPs for a granting organization.

BASIC STEPS FOR WRITING AN RFP AND AWARDING A GRANT

Writing an RFP is essentially the reciprocal of writing a proposal. It addresses the same content and project elements as the proposal, but from a requirements definition aspect rather than a responsive point of view. In other words, the RFP provides the instructions for the grant seeker to follow in submitting a proposal to your organization. A good-quality RFP will increase the probability of your receiving responsive proposals from qualified grant seekers. The same requirements for clear writing style and organization, covered in chapters 9 and 10, apply to RFPs as much as they do to proposals.

RFP CONTENT OUTLINE

The RFP's contents should be sufficiently complete and clear to allow your prospective grantees to determine if they are eligible to receive a grant, what types of projects are eligible for funding, how they may go about applying for a grant, how bidders will be notified of your decision, and how the grant award will be made. Therefore, the RFP should cover these points:

- Background information on the grantor organization, emphasizing its mission and goals related to its granting activities
- Statement of purpose (i.e., specific goals and objectives to be addressed by the solicitation and subsequent proposals)
- Types of projects eligible for grant support
- Target populations of interest
- Geographical limitations
- Institutional grant-eligibility requirements
- Pre-qualification requirements (e.g., letters of intent, etc.)
- Rules for partnering
- Grant cycle schedules (e.g., dates for RFP issue, proposal submission deadline, grant award/rejection, project conclusion)

- Levels and limits of available grant funding, including matching funds requirements
- Number of grants to be made
- Restrictions on use of funds
- Proposal/project evaluation criteria and their weighting
- Evaluation steps (e.g., paper review, oral interviews, etc.)
- Project administrative requirements (e.g., reporting, payment schedules, etc.)
- Proposal specifications (e.g., organization, content, project budget detail, size limitation, format, packaging, mode of submission, number of copies, etc.)
- Proposal budget specifications (e.g., format, degree of detail, allowable costs, etc.)
- Points and conditions of contact between grantor and grantee/grant seeker
- Pre-proposal activities and help (e.g., letters of intent, bidders' conferences, inquiries, etc.)
- Modes of monitoring grant progress and changes of scope
- Grant-awarding procedures, including notification, negotiation, and execution of necessary contractual agreements

Guidelines on establishing proposal content specifications and evaluation criteria may be derived from chapter 10 on writing a proposal section by section. This means that the RFP should give the grant seekers guidance on how they are to present to you the *Why, What, Who, When,* and *How* of their proposed projects. You will need to review your RFP using both in-house and outside experts to ensure its validity. On high-profile projects, be sure to get the input of all interested parties before releasing the RFP.

RFP REVIEW AND PUBLICATION

In addition to designing and writing an RFP, you will have to develop a plan for advertising and distributing the RFP to prospective respondents. You are, in a sense, marketing your need to fund grants to potential grant seekers. In this regard, employ some marketing savvy and title your RFP in a way which is both descriptive and provocative enough to attract the attention and response of the kind of grant seekers you are interested in. I have seen an RFP unimaginatively entitled "Public Library Project Funding" when "Helping Public Libraries Respond to Special Community Needs" might attract more interest and better bidders.

Some grant makers advertise the availability of grants to the public at large via a press release or a notice on a website. Others may limit their solicitations to a preferred bidders list of institutions they believe may be interested or with whom they prefer to work. Others may delegate their RFP announcement to a third party such as the Foundation Center, the American Library Association, or others. You can consider using these and the various channels for announcing the availability of grant RFPs that are reviewed in chapter 4 of this book. Note that some grant-announcing organizations may have specific, formal rules for the advertising of RFPs that must be followed. Make sure that you know which rules apply to your institution.

You can distribute your RFP in traditional hard-copy format or in electronic format, as many grant seekers are now doing. Similarly, you can request proposals be submitted in hard-copy or electronic format or both.

PROPOSAL RECEIPT AND REVIEW

If you are requesting hard-copy proposals, you have the option of specifying mode of delivery such as USPS Priority Mail, parcel delivery such as UPS, or even hand delivery for local bidders.

You will need to develop a methodology and criteria for evaluating the proposals you receive and assemble a team of objective and qualified reviewers to apply the criteria and then rank the applicants. This team should include financial and management professionals as well as programmatic technical specialists to ensure that all aspects of the proposal are thoroughly reviewed. Looking down the pike, you will also need contract personnel to draw up the grant agreements with successful grantees, financial people to issue grant payment checks, and project monitors to keep track of funded grant project progress and to evaluate project results.

Now that you have issued your RFP and set up your review panel, you can sit back and wait for the proposals from grant seekers to arrive. If the grant seekers have read the RFP carefully (paying attention to my rule number 6: *Read the grantor's instructions and give them exactly what they want!*), perhaps they have also employed a grant-writing guide such as this book. Then you may receive responsive proposals that will be worthy of a grant from your institution, and then *let the projects begin!*

Conclusion:
Why Become a Grantsman
(or Grantswoman)?

Because of a struggling economy and resultant reductions in funding, public and other libraries are showing increased interest in grants as a source of supplemental income. Grants can be a particularly important resource for funding special developmental projects that are beyond the reach of tight operating budgets. To a small public library grants are, in a sense, like *pennies from heaven.* They allow a small library with limited means to obtain technology and resources that are normally available only to large, well-funded institutions. I know because I was able to get grants for my small rural public library that funded the purchase of computers and furniture and paid for special community programs. These activities would not have been possible otherwise.

If you master the skills and tools of grantsmanship, then you just might be able to find a grant maker with a need to give that matches your need to receive. You can then submit a proposal for a project of mutual interest, win a grant and, ergo, you are a grantsman or grantswoman. Grant seeking requires one to develop and apply skills in marketing, writing, and project management tempered with creativity and a bit of a gambler's spirit. Once you feel comfortable with grant proposal writing, you may find it to be a game you can win at, which is exciting and rewarding in many ways.

By writing grant proposals on a regular basis, I was able to increase my public library's annual budget by 10 percent and provide my library patrons with many benefits that would not have been attainable otherwise. You can too!

Sample Grantor Prospect Worksheets

Used with permission, copyright the Foundation Center.

FIGURE A.1

FOUNDATION CENTER'S PROSPECT WORKSHEET
FOR INSTITUTIONAL FUNDERS

Date:		
Basic Information		
Name		
Address		
Contact person		
Financial data		
Total assets		
Total grants paid		
Grant ranges/ Amount needed		
Period of funding/ Project		
Is Funder a Good Match?	**Funder**	**Your Organization**
Subject focus (list in order of importance)	1.	1.
	2.	2.
	3.	3.

(cont.)

Geographic limits		
Type(s) of support		
Population(s) served		
Type(s) of recipients		
People (officers, donors, trustees, staff)		

Application Information	
Does the funder have printed guidelines/ application forms?	
Initial approach (letter of inquiry, formal proposal)	
Deadline(s)	
Board meeting date(s)	

Sources of Above Information		
☐ 990-PF—Year:	☐ Requested	☐ Received
☐ Annual report—Year:	☐ Requested	☐ Received
☐ Directories/Grant indexes		
☐ Grantmaker website:		

Notes:

Follow-up:

FOUNDATION CENTER'S PROSPECT WORKSHEET
FOR INDIVIDUAL DONORS

Basic Information
Name (first, middle, last):
Title (Mr., Ms., Mrs., Dr.):
Former or maiden name or nickname:
Address:
Phone number(s):
Alternate address:
Employment Information
Place of employment:
Website (if any): http://
Address:
Work phone number:
Work e-mail:
Position (title):
Since (date):
Salary and other benefits (estimated):
Other relevant employment-related data (former employment):
Personal Information
School(s) attended:
Board affiliations(s):
Foundation affiliation(s) (if any):

(cont.)

Civic/volunteer interests:
Social (include club memberships):
Hobbies:
Giving history (include large gifts, dates, etc.):
Assets (real estate, stock, etc.):
Other wealth indicators:
Family Information (if applicable)
Spouse's name:
Spouse's occupation:
Spouse's affiliation(s):
Spouse's philanthropy:
Children's school(s):
Connection to Your Organization
Board member (dates):
Volunteer (current?):
Current or past donor (amount and other details):
Friend of board member or staff (provide contact name):
Other (shared interests, etc.):
Area(s) of Commonality with the Prospect
Prior giving history:
Geography:
Subject field:

(cont.)

People:
Other:
Sources Consulted (provide URLs, dates, and other details)
Search engines (terms used):
Websites:
Databases:
Contribution lists:
Directories:
Newspapers:
Other:
History of Past Cultivation (if any)
Type (letter, call, invitation, meeting, etc., and dates):
Recommended Next Step(s)
(Indicate deadlines):

APPENDIX

Sample Grant Final Report to a Foundation

Milanof-Schock Library

Serving East Donegal Township, Marietta Borough,
Mount Joy Borough, Mount Joy Township, and Rapho Township

1184 Anderson Ferry Road
Mount Joy, PA 17552-9723

Herbert B. Landau
Library Director
Phone (717) 653-1510
Fax (717) 653- 6590
landau@mountjoy.lib.pa.us

August 6, 2008   VIA E-MAIL

To: Bill & Melinda Gates Foundation

Subject: Final Report on Grant Number XXXX

Dear Ms. YYYY:

The Milanof-Schock Library is pleased to submit this final report as requested by you via telephone on August 4th.

Our report, which follows, is in two parts:

1. Financial Report—Use of Grant Funds

2. Narrative Report

Please do not hesitate to contact me if you require any additional data or have any questions.

We appreciate the generosity of the Gates Foundation and all you do for the world's public libraries.

Sincerely,

Herbert B. Landau
Library Director
Enclosure: Grant XXXX Final Report

FINAL REPORT

Grant Number XXXX

THE BILL & MELINDA GATES FOUNDATION

FOR

BEST SMALL LIBRARY IN AMERICA
2006 AWARD

AUGUST 6, 2006

Milanof-Schock Library

Serving East Donegal Township, Marietta Borough,
Mount Joy Borough, Mount Joy Township,
and Rapho Township

1184 Anderson Ferry Road
Mount Joy, PA 17552
717-653-1510 fax: 717-653-6590
www.mslibrary.org

Submitted by
HERBERT B. LANDAU
LIBRARY DIRECTOR

1. SUMMARY

In February 2006, the Milanof-Schock Library of Mount Joy, Pennsylvania, was named *Best Small Library in America 2006*. As a result, it received a grant from The Gates Foundation in the amount of $13,670.00. Of these funds, $10,000 were employed to improve library services to the Milanof-Schock Library's patrons and $3,670 were employed to cover professional membership and meeting expenses for two library staff members as authorized in The Gates Foundation grant letter of February 13, 2006.

2. FINANCIAL REPORT—USE OF GRANT FUNDS

The table below indicates how the $13,670.00 in grant funding was expended to improve library services and to cover staff professional expenses. The following narrative report will provide more details.

Grant Number XXXXX
FUNDS EXPENDED IN 2006

Purpose	Amount	Impact
Increase Critical Library Staff Hours	$5,203	Increased Circulation/ Technical Services leader hours from ¾ to full-time
Increase Classic and New Adult Book Acquisitions	$3,709	Purchased 179 additional books
Improve Children's Audiovisual Materials	$573	Purchased 30 additional juvenile DVDs to replace VHS
Increase Library Educational Programs	$515	Presented six additional adult and children's programs
ALA/PLA Memberships for Two Staff	$250	Membership for Assistant Director and Community Relations Coordinator
PLA Conference Registration for Two Staff	$420	Registration for Assistant Director and Community Relations Coordinator
PLA Conference Attendance for Two Staff	$3,000	Attendance for Assistant Director and Community Relations Coordinator

3. NARRATIVE REPORT

3.A Use of Grant Funds to Improve Library Services

Of the $13,670 in grant funds received by the Milanof-Schock Library from the Bill & Melinda Gates Foundation in 2006, $10,000 were employed to improve library services to the community we serve. The use of these funds is described below.

3.A.1 Increase Critical Library Staff Hours

At the beginning of 2006, with the exception of the Library Director, all of the Milanof-Schock Library's staff worked on a part-time basis. This situation was the result of limited funds. The critical position of Circulation/Technical Services Coordinator, held by Susan C., was responsible for all circulation, collection maintenance, acquisition, and cataloging functions within the library. However, since this position was funded for only 30 hours per week, some backlogs in key, patron-oriented functions began to develop. By employing $5,203 in Gates Foundation grant funds, we were able to expand this position to full-time (40 hours per week) in 2006, with improved service to library patrons resulting. In 2007 and 2008, we were able to obtain funds to sustain this position at the full-time level.

3.A.2 Increase Classic and New Adult Book Acquisitions

We employed $3,709 in Gates Foundation grant funds to expand our adult fiction and nonfiction book-acquisition program to improve our collections. We began by improving our classic fiction collection, adding books by such authors as Tolstoy, Dickens, Steinbeck, Hemingway, etc., to both fill gaps and to replace worn-out copies. We were also able to improve our nonfiction collection by filling gaps in our biography, American history, and Pennsylvania history holdings. We were also able to acquire several core titles in the area of renewable energy and energy conservation as the nucleus of a new environmental collection. We purchased 179 adult titles with grant funds.

3.A.3 Improve Children's Audiovisual Materials

A very well-used portion of our library's collection is the children's educational and recreational videos. By 2006, our existing collection of VHS-format children's films was largely worn out and becoming obsolescent in the face of increasing patron demands for the DVD format. We were able to replace 30 of our most popular children's VHS videos with DVD-format items using $573 in grant funds.

3.A.4 Increase Library Educational Programs

We employed $515 in grant funding as seed money for six additional adult, youth, and children's educational programs in 2006:

- American Girl (Children)
- Reading Therapy Dog (Children)
- Red Cross Babysitting Course (Youth)
- Spanish for Adults
- Introduction to Computers and MS Word (Adults)
- Baby Boomer Series (Adults) *This program received the 2006 AARP Award of Excellence for Library Programs for Seniors*

3.B Use of Grant Funds for Professional Membership and Meeting Expenses

3.B.1 Professional Memberships

Grant funding of $250 was put toward obtaining annual membership in the Public Library Association of the American Library Association for Milanof-Schock Library Assistant Director Nancy B. and Community Relations Coordinator Greta K.

3.B.2 PLA Conference Registration

Grant funding of $420 was used to defray registration fees at the March 2006 Public Library Association Conference in Boston, MA, for Milanof-Schock Library Assistant Director Nancy B. and Community Relations Coordinator Greta K.

3.B.3 PLA Conference Attendance

Grant funding of $3,000 was used to defray travel and living expenses for the March 2006 Public Library Association Conference in Boston, MA, for Milanof-Schock Library Assistant Director Nancy B. and Community Relations Coordinator Greta K.

Resources on Winning Library Grants

Books

American Library Association. *The Big Book of Library Grant Money 2006: Profiles of Private and Corporate Foundations and Direct Corporate Givers Receptive to Library Grant Proposals.* Chicago: American Library Association, 2006.

Anderson, Cynthia. *Write Grants, Get Money Back.* Santa Barbara, CA: Linworth, 2001.

Barber, Peggy, and Linda D. Crowe. *Getting Your Grant: A How-to-Do-It Manual for Librarians.* New York: Neal-Schuman, 1993.

Boss, Richard W. *Grant Money and How to Get It: A Handbook for Librarians.* New York: Bowker, 1980.

Brown, Larissa Golden. *Demystifying Grant Seeking: What You Really Need to Do to Get Grants.* San Francisco: Jossey-Bass, 2001.

Browning, Beverly A. *Perfect Phrases for Writing Grant Proposals: Hundreds of Ready-to-Use Phrases to Present Your Organization, Explain Your Cause, and Get the Funding You Need.* New York: McGraw-Hill, 2008.

Burkholder, Preethi. *Start Your Own Grant-Writing Business: Your Step-by-Step Guide to Success.* Irvine, CA: Entrepreneur, 2008.

Carlson, Mim, and Tori O'Neal-McElrath. *Winning Grants: Step by Step.* San Francisco: Jossey-Bass, 2008.

Clarke, Cheryl. *Grant Proposal Makeover: Transform Your Request from No to Yes.* San Francisco: Jossey-Bass, 2007.

———. *Storytelling for Grantseekers: The Guide to Creative Nonprofit Fundraising.* San Francisco: Jossey-Bass, 2001.

Collins, Sarah, ed. *The Foundation Center's Guide to Winning Proposals.* New York: Foundation Center, 2006.

Cowan , Kristen Tosh, Melissa Junge, and Sheara Krvaric. *Federal Education Grants Management*. Washington, DC: Thompson, 2009.

Culick, Lisa, Kristen Godard, and Natasha Terk. *The Due Diligence Tool for Use in Pre-Grant Assessment*. Washington, DC: Grantmakers for Effective Organizations, 2004.

Everything Technology: Directory of Technology Grants, Awards, Contests, Grants, Scholarships. New York: Technology Grant News, 2009.

Falkenstein, Jeffrey A. *National Guide to Funding in Health*. 9th ed. New York: Foundation Center, 2005.

_____. *National Guide to Funding in Religion*. 8th ed. New York: Foundation Center, 2005.

Federal Grants Management Handbook. Washington, DC: Thompson, 2009.

Frey, Robert S. *Successful Proposal Strategies for Small Businesses: Using Knowledge Management to Win Government, Private-Sector, and International Contracts*. Norwood, MA: Artech House, 2009.

Gerding, Stephanie, and Pam MacKellar. *Grants for Libraries: A How-to-Do-It Manual*. New York: Neal-Schuman, 2006.

Gitlin, Laura N., and Kevin Lyons. *Successful Grant Writing: Strategies for Health and Human Service*. 3rd ed. New York: Springer, 2009.

Guide to Federal Funding for Government and Nonprofits. Washington, DC: Thompson, 2009.

Hall, Mary, and Susan Howlett. *Getting Funded: The Complete Guide to Writing Grant Proposals*. 4th ed. Portland, OR: Continuing Education Press, Portland State University, 2003.

Hall-Ellis, Sylvia D., and Ann Jerabek. *Grants for School Libraries*. Santa Barbara, CA: Libraries Unlimited, 2003.

Hall-Ellis, Sylvia D., Doris Meyer, Frank W. Hoffmann, and Judy Ann Jerabek, ed. Frank W. Hoffmann. *Grantsmanship for Small Libraries and School Library Media Centers*. Santa Barbara, CA: Libraries Unlimited, 1999.

Holtzclaw, Barbara, Carole Kenner, and Marlene Walden, eds. *Grant Writing Handbook for Nurses*. 2nd ed. Sudbury, MA: Jones and Bartlett, 2009.

Jacobs, David G., ed. *Foundation Directory 2009*. New York: Foundation Center, 2009.

Kruger, Richard A., and Mary Anne Richards. *Focus Groups: A Practical Guide for Applied Research*. 4th ed. Newbury Park, CA: Pine Forge, 2008.

Margolin, Judith B., and Elan K. DiMaio, eds. *Grantseeker's Guide to Winning Proposals*. New York: Foundation Center, 2008.

Miner, Jeremy T., and Lynn E. Miner. *Proposal Planning and Writing.* Westport, CT: Greenwood, 2008.

New, Cheryl Carter. *Grantseeker's Toolkit: A Comprehensive Guide to Finding Funding.* New York: J. Wiley, 1998.

Perspectives on Outcome Based Evaluation for Libraries and Museums. Washington, DC: Institute of Museum and Library Services, n.d.

Quick, James Aaron. *Grant Seeker's Budget Toolkit.* New York: John Wiley, 2001.

Smith, Nancy Burke, and E. Gabriel Works. *The Complete Book of Grant Writing: Learn to Write Grants like a Professional.* Naperville, IL: Sourcebooks, 2006.

Stinson, Karen, and Phyl Renninger. *Collaboration in Grant Development and Management.* Washington, DC: Thompson, 2009.

_____. *Questions and Answers for the Grants Professional: Achieving Excellence.* Washington, DC: Thompson, 2009.

_____. *References in Grant Development and Management.* Washington, DC: Thompson, 2009.

Teitel, Martin. *Thank You for Submitting Your Proposal: A Foundation Director Reveals What Happens Next.* Medfield, MA: Emerson & Church, 2006.

Ward, Deborah, ed. *Writing Grant Proposals That Win.* 3rd ed. Sudbury, MA: Jones and Bartlett, 2006.

Wells, Michael K. *Grantwriting beyond the Basics. Book 1: Proven Strategies Professionals Use to Make Their Proposals Work.* Portland, OR: Continuing Education Press, Portland State University, 2005.

_____. *Grantwriting beyond the Basics. Book 2, Understanding Nonprofit Finances.* Portland, OR: Continuing Education Press, Portland State University, 2006.

_____. *Grantwriting beyond the Basics. Book 3, Successful Program Evaluation.* Portland, OR: Continuing Education Press, Portland State University, 2007.

_____. *Proven Strategies Professionals Use to Make Their Proposals Work.* Portland, OR: Continuing Education Press, Portland State University, 2005.

Winning at It: Grant Writing for Technology Grants; Corporate & Government Tech Grants, with Winning Proposals & Projects for Non-Profits; K-12 Schools, Colleges & Universities, Individuals, Awards, Fellowships with Winning Proposals, Projects. New York: Technology Grant News, 2009.

Online Resources

There are a variety of online information resources available to help you iden-tify potential grants. You will get the most up-to date information online. Using a web crawler such as Bing, Google, or Metacrawler, you can search under "library grants" and find quite a few sources of information. The following is a listing of some grant-finding Internet websites that I have found useful.

ALA Scholarship Program grants. www.ala.org/ala/awardsgrants/grants/index
.cfm.

Catalog of Federal Domestic Assistance. www.cfda.gov.

The Chronicle's Guide to Grants. Subscription list of U.S. foundation and corporate grants. www.philanthropy.com.

Council on Foundations. www.cof.org.

Dun & Bradstreet. Here you may apply for a DUNS number. http://www.dnb
.com/US/duns_update.

Economic Recovery Grants Center. www.grantsinfocenter.com/resources.

Education World Grants Newsletter. Education World publishes this free grants newsletter biweekly. www.educationworld.com/maillist.shtml.

Federal Register. www.gpoaccess.gov/fr/index.html.

Foundation Center. www.foundationcenter.org.

Foundation Grants for Preservation in Libraries, Archives, and Museums. www.loc.gov/preserv/foundtn-grants.pdf.

Grants for Libraries Hotline. Subscription service offering weekly updates on grant opportunities and instruction on grant writing. http://west.thomson. com/productdetail/139015/40560036/productdetail.aspx.

Grants.gov. Central source for U.S. federal government grants. www
.grants.gov.

Grantsmanship Center's Funding Sources Guide. State guides to grant-making foundations, corporate giving programs, community foundations, and state government home pages. http://tgci.com/abouthistory.shtml.

GrantSmart. Uses IRS Form 990 tax return reports to compile a database currently containing 625,350 tax returns filed by 104,060 private foundations. www.grantsmart.org.

GrantsWire. Subscription announcement service for grant opportunities of federal agencies and foundations. www.thompson.com.

GuideStar. Forms 990-PF information on 1.8 million nonprofit organizations. www.guidestar.org.

Internet Library for Librarians. The "Library Grants Section" provides links to grant-writing resources, search engines for grant resources, sites providing funding for projects, grant proposal guides and forms, and charitable foundations' policy information. www.itcompany.com/inforetriever/grant .htm.

The Library Grants Blog. Listings of current library grant solicitations from a variety of organizations. www.librarygrants.blogspot.com.

Michigan State University, Grants for Individuals: Library and Information Science. http://staff.lib.msu.edu/harris23/grants/3libsci.htm.

National Center for Charitable Statistics at the Urban Institute. http:// nccsdataweb.urban.org/PubApps/990search.php.

Recovery.gov. The U.S. government's official website to access American Recovery and Reinvestment Act grants. www.recovery.gov.

School Funding Center grant database. Subscription database and new-letter service oriented toward education grants. www.schoolfunding center .info.

Technology and Learning Online. Searchable database of grant, scholarship, and other funding opportunities for educators and students. www .techlearning.com.

Technology Grant News and *Grant Index.* A subscription-service index to grants for libraries and museums. www.technologygrantnews.com.

U.S. Office of Management and Budget. Federal grant forms. www .whitehouse.gov/omb/grants/grants_forms.html.

University of North Carolina, Grants for Library Science Students. http:// research.unc.edu/grantsource/library_science.php.

University of Wisconsin-Madison, Grants Information Center Resources for Nonprofit Organizations. http://grants.library.wisc.edu.

Periodicals

A good place to start looking for grant-oriented periodicals is the University of Wisconsin-Madison Libraries' Grants Information Collection website, which offers an excellent, up-to-date listing of "Philanthropy Periodicals and News" at http://grants.library.wisc.edu/organizations/newsletters.html.

In print format, you can consult the biweekly *Chronicle of Grants* (www .philanthropy.com), a spin-off of the *Chronicle of Philanthropy* newspaper for not-for-profits which monitors the grant scene. Its subscribers can also access the Chronicle's Guide to Grants database, which endeavors to list all available U.S. foundation and corporate grants. The Foundation Center's *Philanthropy News Digest* (*PND*) announces RFPs and notices of awards as a free service for grant-making organizations and nonprofits. The Foundation Center also issues the weekly *PND RFP Bulletin* via e-mail at no charge to subscribers. Both of these free services are available through the Foundation Center's website: http:// foundationcenter.org/pnd/rfp. *{Centered}: News for Grantseekers* is an e-zine published monthly by the Grantsmanship Center which provides useful articles for grant seekers and proposal writers, as well as expert advice from the Grants- manship Center's trainers: www.tgci.com/newsletter/index.asp. *Fund$Raiser Cyberzine* (www.fundsraiser.com) is a free online magazine for small as well as large nonprofits. The online version of the *Grantsmanship Center Magazine* (www.tgci.com/magazine.shtml) contains the full-text articles published by this quarterly newsletter, which is available free to members of nonprofits.

Index